Your Shift Matters

Discover How 25 Amazing People Turned Burnouts and Breakdowns into Breakthroughs

Compiled by

Dana Zarcone

For more information, visit:

Compiler / Publisher: www.danazarcone.com

Book and cover design by: Jennifer Insignares www.yourdesignsbyjen.com

Editing by: Amanda Horan www.amandahoranediting.com

Formatting by: Bojan Kratofil https://facebook.com/bojan.kratofil

ISBN: 978-1-5136-2372-6

Gratitude Page

First and foremost, I want to start by showing my appreciation for all the authors of this book who, like myself, have a passion for inspiring others and understand that this book is a powerful way to make this happen. Some of you are long-time friends, while others I'm just getting to know. Either way, I couldn't be more blessed or grateful to have you on this journey with me. I know some, if not all of you, are taking a big risk. Maybe you're revealing yourself in a way that's never been shared before, or you're telling a story that's never been told before. Either way, I feel so much gratitude that you decided to join me on this journey. I know that you'll impact so many lives through the stories you share. Thank you! I hope that this journey has been as amazing for you as it has been for me!

The past few years have been full of some serious ups and downs. Some of which I'm sure I'll write about in future books. For now, suffice it to say I wouldn't be where I am today without so many beautiful friends in my life. People who support me, love me and even give me a swift, well-needed kick in the keister at times. Some of whom are authors of this book! Uh, you know who you are! Big hugs to you!

In addition, one person that had a big influence in my life is my mother. She's been my biggest cheerleader! My mom always encouraged me to follow my dreams and to never give up! I'm dating myself here, but maybe you've heard of the *Regis and Kathy Lee Show*? Well, Kathy Lee eventually decided to leave the show, and they were looking for a replacement. I think I was in my early twenties at the time, with absolutely no experience in that industry, but my mom was convinced that I was a shoo-in as her replacement! That's how much she believed in me! Unfortunately, she passed away in 2008. However, I know that she's still cheering me on from above. Thanks, Mom, for everything! I love you, and I miss you so, so much!

I would be remiss not to include my dad as well. This section is about expressing my gratitude, and I am so grateful to him! He's always been very supportive. However, he's also played a pivotal role picking up the slack since my mom's passing. Whenever I need a shoulder to cry on (literally) he's always there for me! He's proof that, no matter how old you are, you still need a parent to lean on and guide you along the way sometimes. I love you, Dad! Thank you for being there for me and helping to make this dream come true! I couldn't have done it without you!

Finally, I am so grateful for my husband and two daughters who have sacrificed a lot for me. Thank you all very much for your love and support. I hope that I'm able to inspire you, as my mom inspired me, to follow your dreams and never give up! And, never forget, *Your Shift Matters!*

Table of Contents

Foreword

The saying 'The desires of your heart will be answered, but it takes you to notice the signs of their arrival' is so powerful. It is up to you to become highly aware of the possibilities and make them a reality.

That is exactly what Dana did when she had the desire to bring these amazing people together to share their stories. She's made her dream come true and has touched so many lives as a result.

My journey with Dana over the last year or so has been very powerful. She has taught me things that she won't even realize until she reads this foreword. She has taught me how a student embraces a learning journey, leaving no stone unturned and translating what has been taught to her in her own unique and powerful way to her own co-authors.

That's what this entire journey is about. We must take what somebody has taught us and then decide how we can place our unique footprint upon it so that it is completed in a unique style, and that's exactly what Dana did.

When I started out with my own group project in 2012, I never thought in a million years that it would be the seed planted for Dana's journey, and the book that lies before you now. You see, you can plant seeds in your life now, but you have no clue what fruit will reap from that seed years down the line. That's why it's so important to *never* give up!

No matter how dark times may seem, even if you feel you can't go on, you *must*! You have greatness within you that is stronger than anything on this planet. This book is a true example of that power; the power of souls who have come back from experiences that will shock you, astound you and get your heart pumping.

Experiences that inspire you to keep going and reach deep down into the depths of your soul to awaken something strong within you.

A journey of self-discovery is a powerful one that will shift you with all your might. It will test you, change you, and make you see things that you never thought possible. The most important thing you will realize is that *Your Shift Matters*.

Dana, I am extremely proud of you and your co-authors for making this book a reality. Here's to all of you creating a legacy and making your families proud too!

It's been my true honor to see this book come alive! I wish you all amazing success!

Much love and appreciation,

Kate Gardner.

18 x best-selling author, publishing consultant and creator of The Missing Piece Magazine.

www.themissingpiecemagazine.com

www.ayearofchange.com

Dana's Introduction

Welcome to the beginning of an amazing journey! This is the first book in the Your Shift Matters book series that is sure to inspire, motivate and move you in ways you've never felt before. This series brings authors together from all over the world who share raw and real stories of overcoming unimaginable challenges, rising strong, and learning many lessons along the way. Their stories are sure to challenge your mind, touch your heart, and ignite your spirit.

When I started my podcast 'Your Shift Matters', I never thought in a million years that it would lead me down this powerful path of creating a book series. The underlying message in all of my work is that you have to deal with your shit in order to make a shift!

This is something that I'm very passionate about as I've seen and experienced a lot of suffering, as have the authors of this book. I'm certain you've experienced your fair share of suffering as well. This breaks my heart because we suffer needlessly! We aren't meant to suffer. Rather we're supposed to feel vibrantly alive, resonating with love, joy, and compassion. We're meant to live a fulfilling, meaningful life. Yet, the majority of us don't live this way. Instead, we suffer needlessly; some even suffer endlessly.

In this book, the authors get raw and real and unveil their suffering to you. They share their stories of overcoming adversity, facing tough challenges and shifting from burnouts and breakdowns to breakthroughs. They share the pain, heartbreak, agony, grief, sorrow, and suffering they've endured. They expose their underbellies in the spirit of helping you understand that we all go through hard times, no one is immune, and everyone can come out on the other side, stronger, wiser and happier than ever before!

Through their stories, they will inspire you and give you hope. They will give you a sense of knowingness that if they can overcome the pain they've had to endure, anyone can!

I invite you to read each story without judgment; with an open heart and genuine compassion. By approaching each chapter with an open mind, it's my suspicion that you will find a little bit of yourself in each of these stories. You will realize that you, too, can move from burnouts and breakdowns to your own personal breakthroughs. As you read each of these stories, I hope you realize that when you're suffering there's nothing to be ashamed of - there's nothing to fear.

You see, shame and fear are very close friends, and they will keep you stuck. When you feel shame about your struggles, and you're afraid to make a change, you will be forever condemned to burnouts and breakdowns. As a result, a breakthrough won't be possible.

I'm passionate about this because so many people suffer, stay stuck, and live unhappy lives if for no other reason than they refuse to deal with their shit! Are you one of them? I was guilty of this for a very long time. I'm sure my authors have been guilty of this as well. Instead of dealing with the issue - or perhaps more importantly - the pain associated with the issue, everything is swept under the rug or pushed aside in hopes it will all go away; It won't. When it doesn't, we're quick to look outside ourselves for the easy button, happy pill, or magic potion that will make it all better.

Through my education, personal experience and working with hundreds of clients across the globe, I am convinced now more than ever that quick fixes aren't sustainable. They won't help you make the life-changing shift that you want to make. Instead, you have to deal with your shit in order to make a shift, just like the authors of this book have.

Are you ready for a breakthrough?

It's through my podcast, this book and the amazing stories the authors share that you'll find the hope, inspiration, and determination to do what you need to do turn your burnouts and breakdowns into breakthroughs!

Remember, at the end of the day, in order to live your life all in and full out, *Your Shift Matters*!

With lots of heartfelt love and gratitude,

Dana Zarcone

The 'Liberating Leadership Coach'.

Coach | Trainer | Best-Selling Author | Publisher | Motivational Speaker

www.danazarcone.com

www.yourshiftmatters.com

Dana Zarcone

Dana Zarcone, known as 'The Liberating Leadership Coach', is passionate about helping her clients live all in and full out, step into their power, and enjoy epic success in life and business. Following a successful twenty-four year corporate career, Dana earned her master's degree in counseling. She works as a national certified counselor, certified Core Energetics practitioner, certified kinesiologist and leadership coach. Dana is the founder of Liberating Leadership Solutions™ - a company that provides leadership training as well as individual and group coaching. She's a coach, trainer, motivational speaker, international best-selling author, and host of the *Your Shift Matters* podcast

Learn more about Dana:

www.DanaZarcone.com

www.YourShiftMatters.com

www.Facebook.com/SourceYourJoy

Chapter 1

People 'Like Me'

By Dana Zarcone

It's 2:30 in the morning and I can feel the cold tiles underneath me as I lie on the bathroom floor bawling my eyes out. My heart is breaking into a million pieces. I can feel the immense pressure on my chest, making it difficult to breathe. I have no strength to hold myself up anymore, so I'm simply lying here limp and lifeless. My whole world is falling apart. I'm falling apart.

I'm listening to a Whitney Houston song; *I Look to You*. It says, "As I lay me down, heaven hear me now. I'm lost without a cause, after giving it my all. Winter storms have come and darkened my sun. After all that I've been through, who on earth can I turn to? I look to you."

As I'm listening to it, I'm pleading with God to bring me home. No, actually, I'm *begging* God to bring me home; I'm done. I can't do this anymore. I can't go on living this way anymore.

I hit my personal rock bottom, and I hit it *hard*! I seriously don't know what else to do. I'm experiencing gut-wrenching pain. Pain, unlike anything I've ever felt before. I'm feeling an overwhelming sense of sadness, grief, and despair. I feel hopeless and helpless. I'm exhausted from the struggle. I don't want to suffer anymore.

I want to be saved. I want God to bring me home. *Please bring me home!*

I now know what it feels like to have a broken heart. Ironically, my broken heart isn't the result of a relationship breakup or death in the family. It's the result of pure exhaustion. Exhaustion from pretending to be someone I'm not.

I know that, in many ways, I've turned my life over to other people. My husband, parents, children, family, friends — everyone. I would acquiesce in big ways (not speaking up when someone hurt me) and in small ways (letting them choose the restaurant). Eventually, this resulted in living a life that wasn't really mine. I'm sacrificing myself in order to meet others' expectations— or what I perceived to be their expectations — leaving me with no sense of *self*. Without knowing my *self*, I have no real emotional strength, confidence or sense of self-worth.

Growing up, I had a history of being betrayed by the people who were close to me. People I trusted. People I thought had my best interest at heart. I'm sure each of those experiences will end up in future books. For now, suffice it to say that all of these experiences brought me deep pain. Pain that I never fully acknowledged, much less processed. From these experiences, I concluded that I wasn't good enough, wasn't lovable, and didn't matter.

Looking back, I know that I made this up. I took my experiences and the pain from those experiences and made them mean something about me. No one told me that I wasn't enough, I wasn't lovable or that I didn't matter. I came to that conclusion all on my own. As a little girl, it was the only conclusion I could come to that made any sense.

These false, limiting beliefs were imprinted on my subconscious mind so early in my developmental years that they ruled my life.

My self-esteem had diminished to a record low. As a result, I organized my life around proving to everyone, including myself, that the opposite was true.

I went to college, got great grades and landed a really high paying job with a large Fortune 100 company. I relied heavily on the environment to prove my worth to myself and everyone around me. I had an important job title, great paycheck, nice car, a yacht, and a house with a white picket fence. Well, ok, no picket fence, but you get the idea!

I was an eager-to-please woman running on a treadmill to nowhere land. I compulsively burned the candle at both ends (as my parents used to say), impressing everyone with my ability to juggle impossible tasks. I was overextended and overcommitted and, looking back, I realize it was to avoid facing how unhappy I really was. How unhappy I was with myself, my marriage, my role as a mother, my life in general.

In this state of avoidance, I wore a mask that I presented to the world. I was seen as a real ambitious, fun-loving, laid-back, successful go-getter. Yet, on the inside, it wasn't how I felt at all. I felt insecure, afraid and unsure. In fact, I felt like a fraud. I suppose in some ways, I actually *was* a fraud. I certainly wasn't shouting from the rooftops that I felt unlovable; I had a low sense of self-worth and felt like crap most days. Of course not! If people knew how I was really feeling they'd judge me and see me as weak, broken, 'less than'. They'd abandon me. At least, that's what I believed at the time.

As a result, what I was shouting from the rooftops was 'look how successful I am, look at how fun-loving and compassionate I am'. I positioned myself as someone who was strong, independent and could handle anything that came my way! As if I was somehow above it all. Above the pain and suffering, above the drama and trauma – above it all.

This attitude led to what I affectionately call PLMS. No, not PMS. Although I'm sure that got in my way many times as well! I had PLMS (people 'like me' syndrome). People 'like me' don't get raped. People 'like me' don't suffer from depression. People 'like me' don't have anxiety attacks. People 'like me' don't get abused. People 'like me' don't rely on liquid courage to get through life. Guess what? People like me *do*… and I *did*.

I've had many traumatic experiences in my life. However, because I was above it all, and could handle anything, I simply picked myself up, brushed myself off and went on my merry way. Obviously, that was a defense mechanism. I was in denial, and as a result, I never fully processed the pain. I never dealt with all the anger, rage, sadness, longing, guilt, and shame I was feeling. Instead, I buried it. I buried it so deep; I fully expected I'd never have to deal with it again.

Unfortunately, it doesn't work that way. The demons and dragons sit on the sidelines, watching and waiting for the perfect time to rear their ugly heads. As the saying goes: you can run, but you can't hide. Eventually, it catches up to you.

I compare it to a pressure cooker. You put the lid on nice and tight so nothing can get out, put it on the stove and turn on the heat. However, it can only take so much heat (this thing called life) before it gets to be too much, the lid blows off, and you've got a huge mess!

This is what happened to me. All the pain I had ignored over the years had come back with a vengeance, and I ended up having a complete breakdown in the middle of the night on the cold tiles of a bathroom floor.

Honestly, this experience was my turning point. It was my wake-up call that something was horribly wrong. I had no sense of self, and my personal power lay dormant. I couldn't be happy because I denied my heart and was overwhelmed with piles of unhealed emotions, limiting core beliefs, visceral fears, and a lot of resistance.

So, how did I make the shift?

Bottom line, I had to deal with my shit! Hence, *Your Shift Matters*!

Contrary to what we'd like to believe, there aren't any easy buttons or happy pill solutions. None that are sustainable long-term anyway. Sure, they may bring about some relief and take the edge off, but in the end, they don't resolve the overarching issue that stems from our beliefs, thoughts, and feelings.

I had a friend once say, "You can only go as high as you're willing to go deep." From my personal and professional experience, I believe this to be true. It's important to look within, or you'll do without – without genuine happiness or a real sense of fulfillment in life.

There are five areas I had to focus on in order to make the S.H.I.F.T. and I'd like to share them with you.

Surrender to the Truth

"You can't change what you don't acknowledge."

-Anonymous

I learned the hard way. I can't change what I don't acknowledge. So, it's important to surrender to the truth, the whole truth and nothing but the truth and do it with love, kindness, and self-compassion.

I needed to acknowledge that something wasn't working in my life. In what area of my life am I unhappy or stuck? Is there something I continue to struggle with but I've done nothing to change it? I learned I couldn't ignore my issues and hope that one day they will magically work themselves out because they won't.

It's human nature to resist change until things get so bad we can't take it anymore; until we're so far down that slippery slope that 'business as usual' isn't an option anymore. Or worse, we wait for a tragedy to strike. I certainly know this first-hand - remember the bathroom floor!?

When we suppress and repress things, they build up in power and intensity and eventually wreak havoc in our lives. If our feelings go unexpressed, they will have a stranglehold on us.

Conversely, if we see the truth and we're honest with ourselves about what we believe and think, how we feel, and why we feel the way we do, we empower ourselves to make the changes that need to be made. To align with our genius and our destiny, we need to surrender to the truth.

Heal Emotional Wounds

"We live our lives at the level of our wounds, not the level of our potential."

-Dana Zarcone

It's our natural instinct to sweep things under the rug and bury the pain of the past by relying on our external environment for relief. However, when emotional pain isn't fully processed it will sabotage our ability to be truly happy and fulfilled.

Whenever we feel unfulfilled, stuck, unable (or unwilling) to change, unhealed emotional wounds are getting in the way. When

12

we have unhealed wounds, we have a very limited idea of who we really are and our capabilities.

In an ideal situation, emotions are felt, processed and 'let go'. Emotions are pure energy. E-motion or energy in motion. So, when emotions aren't fully processed, they become lodged in our bodies and block our energy flow. This affects us emotionally and physically and is responsible for the majority of our imbalances, pain, and diseases. So, it's important to heal emotional wounds, so they don't block the flow; so they don't eventually rear their ugly heads and wreak havoc on our lives!

Identify Underlying Core Beliefs

"You begin to fly when you let go of underlying core beliefs and let your mind soar to new heights."

-Dana Zarcone

Underlying core beliefs are *under* our conscious awareness. They *lie* to us about who we are. Since they're hidden, we're unaware of the extent that they rule our lives. They ultimately dictate what we experience and emerge as unconsciously motivated actions that may or may not be in our best interest.

To change our lives, we must fundamentally change the way we think, act and feel because this forms our personalities which, ultimately, creates our *personal realities.*

Did you know that our conscious mind is only 5% of our intelligence? The conscious mind is where we rationalize, use logic and reasoning and is where our will and intentions come from. The other 95% is our subconscious mind, which is where our core beliefs and perceptions about the world and our sense of self resides. This determines our state of being and drives our patterns of behaviors, actions and, ultimately, our results.

If we want to make a sustainable change in our lives – if we want to change our state of being – we can't do it from the conscious mind. We need to tap into the subconscious mind and reprogram it just as we would a computer. The good news is that through modalities like quantum physics and kinesiology we can do this successfully and transform our lives permanently.

Face Your Fear

"Living with fear stops you from taking risks, and if you don't take risks, you'll never achieve your dreams."

-Dana Zarcone

Oh yes, such a small, little, seemingly harmless word but this is a force to be reckoned with! Gone unnoticed and left to its own demise, we'll be stuck in an unhappy, unbearable limbo land forever!

Fear is a tool used by the ego. The ego is organized around trying to protect us and keep us from being hurt, and fear is one of its many tools used to keep us safe. Ironically, it does just the opposite. It keeps us separate and stuck in bizarre patterns of behavior, making poor choices, and getting undesirable results.

Until we face our fear, we will be used by our ego in destructive ways. Some will be subtle and some not so subtle at all.

There are many ways that fear shows up in our lives. When we're feeling a lot of fear, anger, confusion, resistance, depression, anxiety, exhaustion, addiction, and resentment... these are all faces of fear. It's important to recognize when it's present (see the truth) and face it head-on.

Most of us have learned to *beware of* fear when what we should be doing is *being aware of* it. By exploring our fear, and how we act as a result, we can transform it into positive, forward moving energy.

Transform Your Energy

"Once your energy is transformed, everything is in the realm of possibility."

- Dana Zarcone

As quantum scientists have now proven, *everything* is energy. Everything, including our beliefs, thoughts, emotions, and our bodies. In essence, we are conscious energy with access to infinite possibilities in our lives.

We each resonate at a certain energetic vibration, a frequency if you will. The higher our energetic vibration, the more connected we are to a higher power. The more conscious we are, the easier we manifest abundance in our lives. The more peace, love, and joy we'll feel, the more fulfilled we'll be.

Where we generally vibrate depends on our beliefs, thoughts, and emotions since they are all forms of energy. For instance, I was holding onto unresolved feelings of guilt, shame, grief, and fear, so I was vibrating at a very low frequency. As a result, I felt depressed, hopeless, worried, and anxious. I was playing the victim and blaming others for how miserable I was.

Conversely, when I vibrate at a high level I generally feel acceptance, love, peace, and joy. When this is my experience, I'm approaching life from my heart, intuition and a sense of knowingness that all is as it should be. I'm not a victim or blaming others. Instead, I'm a conscious co-creator in my life.

If we don't transform our energy, our lives will remain the same because we can't change our lives at the same energetic frequency with which we created it.

So there you have it! By focusing on these five areas and dealing with my shit, I was able to make a shift!

See the truth.

Heal your emotional wounds.

Identify underlying core beliefs.

Face your fear.

Transform your energy.

It's not easy, but it's also nowhere near as scary, painful, or life-threatening as we make it out to be. If we surrender to the truth, heal emotional wounds, identify and transform our underlying limiting beliefs and face our fear, we'll transform our energy. We'll vibrate at a higher level, and we'll feel more love, joy, and peace in our lives. We'll avoid having a breakdown on a bathroom floor, begging God to bring us home.

Bevan Bird

Bevan Bird's quest is to create a world where work is joyful and comes from love – for that is what we are all made of.

An entrepreneur, teacher, consultant, and media personality, he helps teachers of higher consciousness build a solid and sustainable online business aligned with their soul's purpose, and grow it using the most powerful marketing strategies — including joint ventures — so they can live their dreams.

With a foot in both worlds, he is a student of conscious evolution and direct-response copywriting. He is passionate, and a great listener who wants you to win!

Learn more about Bevan:

Website: http://PositionOnPurpose.com

Facebook: https://www.facebook.com/birdify

Twitter: https://twitter.com/birdify

Chapter 2

Aimless to Purposeful

By Bevan Bird

In high school, I wanted to fit in with my group of friends. We smoked pot, skateboarded, shoplifted and rebelled against society. Eventually, I was caught shoplifting at a grocery store, so I had to clean out the dumpster as a punishment to avoid getting a criminal record. This was a turning point in my life. I decided to change my evil ways.

Once I graduated high school, my mom said I would have to earn a living. At first, I took the only jobs I could get without experience, which was as a construction laborer, a roofer's helper, and then a grocery clerk.

I decided to try out surveying because I loved being in nature and I have a mathematical gift. I took Saturday courses at BCIT (British Columbia Institute of Technology) and did very well. So in the spring of 2005, I started working at a surveying firm and enrolled in the diploma program at BCIT that fall.

However, by 2009, I found myself in an unfulfilling job. Although I had chosen it using my mathematical gift, which was a step in the right direction (as I believe we should all use our gifts in our work and be celebrated and valued for who we are), it was no longer meeting my need to grow. Like most employees, I was disengaged, with no greater purpose than to earn a daily wage.

I yearned for a meaningful life with growth and adventures.

I also struggled with a core values conflict. It was sickening to work for companies that valued profits but not the health of people and the planet. I wanted to be myself rather than sell my soul to survive.

The job took me out of town a lot, preventing me from having a fulfilling romantic relationship, which is very important to me. The men I worked with didn't have great relationships. I knew if I stayed there, I'd end up like them.

I didn't want to keep living this lonely, boring life.

I felt like I was wasting it. I knew I was meant to be something great.

I was frustrated. I didn't even feel like a whole person. It made me mad. I wanted to make my life an exciting adventure worth making a movie about. Otherwise, what's the point of living?

When I read *The Monk Who Sold His Ferrari* by Robin Sharma, I became inspired to stop accumulating possessions and make my life about enjoying enriching experiences, growing and contributing.

I learned how to meditate. One time, while meditating in the spring of 2010, an infinite force took over within me. I felt as if I was being breathed by God or my highest self instead of me doing the breathing. Like a drop merging with the ocean, I felt everything merge into one living thing. I, as I had known myself, had disappeared and this felt extremely peaceful and blissful. It was a kind of spiritual awakening. Like my dad had told me about his first experience with magic mushrooms, I had become intimate with the infinite in that moment. From that point forward, I have been guided, and I know that I am one with all of life.

I searched my soul for who I wanted to be. I realized I wanted to inspire people.

I quit my job and tried to become an entrepreneur. I would have to learn many lessons before I became successful.

On this new path, I soon got into debt and had to let go of things I held dear: possessions, comfort, plenty of money and a romantic relationship, to get on the right path.

I was evicted from the house I was renting for the past ten years. Luckily, I didn't become homeless; my dad gave me a place to live and food to eat. While there, I learned to be resourceful.

By studying free material online, I discovered joint ventures, which I wanted to leverage immediately but didn't have any money for training.

I felt guilty about having so much debt and letting people down. My financial future looked bleak, and I considered filing for bankruptcy.

However, my energy shifted once I stopped feeling guilty about the debt.

Then I made a major change, which led to my freedom. I had to think and act differently. It felt uncomfortable at first, but it was well worth it! Combining my experience, skills, and aptitudes, I positioned myself as a developer of custom software for geomatics professionals. Basically, I specialized in something I was great at, which was rare and therefore valued more highly by the market.

I shared software online and reached out to my network to discover their needs. Within three weeks I was hired as a geomatics technologist again. I earned $65 an hour and repaid all my debts ($31,000) within four months – that felt amazing!

That summer, I returned to Vancouver. The next March, I rented a luxury Coal Harbour apartment with a view of the Pacific Ocean, the mountains, and Stanley Park. I'd wanted to wake up to this for the last ten years!

I had successfully positioned myself for the first time, improving my life. But I wasn't fulfilled by 'quick and dirty money'. (Money earned by selling something one knows he can do, but not something that he enjoys doing.)

I wanted to enjoy what I do every day. So in 2014, I started investing my surplus where I'd get the best return: self-education.

Soon I discovered my 'sacred gifts': teaching, knowledge, wisdom, and encouragement. I'd use my strengths as I crafted my dream career.

Connecting with experts at marketing conferences, I assembled the tools I needed to succeed.

From Frank Kern, I learned that 'you will be paid for your position in the marketplace'. I learned to maximize my income by choosing my teaching topic strategically, specializing, writing the book on it, and building celebrity. This was something I had to learn. In 2011, I didn't know this, and it's a big reason why I didn't earn enough money to pay the bills.

One thing Sean Mize, the creator of the simplest group coaching model, said made a great impact on me: "Until you know your purpose, you're probably not going to sell very much."

So I closed my eyes, imagined my perfect world, and then I wrote about it. I repeated this process for twenty minutes.

A positive world where everyone does what they love, uses their gifts, appreciates their worth and is valued fairly and celebrated for the unique, brilliant and beautiful being that they are!

This aligned me to my true purpose and inspired me. I could create as much content as I wanted!

Things started to move. I took action, created and marketed information products, got clients, worked with them, and we all grew together.

Your purpose is an intersection of what you love to do, are gifted in, can be paid for and what the world needs. Living on purpose, you become a force of nature.

What exactly will you teach and to whom? What will it do for them? How will it change their lives? How will you actually position yourself as the authority and earn profits by teaching your passion? For example, you could shoot daily videos, write a newsletter, blog posts, articles on popular websites, get interviewed, start a podcast, write a book… all on the specialized topic of your choice.

I created my website Position On Purpose, so I could help people identify their passion and purpose and then profit while making a meaningful difference in the world. However, I didn't build the site for two years. I didn't know at the time that this would be my most important work.

In July 2015, I was surveying a dam rebuild and was feeling depressed because I was neglecting my higher purpose and not living up to my potential. Having a full-time job, I couldn't host a weekly scheduled call, but I decided not to let my circumstances hold me back anymore.

Based on what my tribe wanted to learn, I launched the Tribe Building Mastermind and got five clients in three days. Life became exciting and meaningful again because I could guide people towards success. I felt positive, whole and self-directed again. I had learned an important lesson.

Sean offered to launch a product I would create to his list, which we did just before 2015 ended. I promised to let people watch me connect with 1,111 people over the first ninety days of 2016, and then experienced the power of joint ventures first hand, gaining seventy new clients within a few days.

It felt really good to see that people wanted to learn tribe building and people connecting from me. It was an external validation. I'd learned another important lesson: if you want to sell, don't create what you think is cool. Create a solution to your customers' biggest problem. Meet their every need.

Seeing all the emails from PayPal, I felt excited and saw great potential in joint ventures.

After connecting with all the new people, I was finally certified as a joint venture broker, dealmaker, and consultant by Sohail Khan (one of the world's top three joint venture experts) four years after I first got excited about joint ventures.

Even so, I still suffered a stubbornly recurring pattern: health and wealth didn't seem to go together. I was getting almost no exercise with the cold, rainy weather. I was out of shape. My business wasn't growing fast enough. Working most of the time, I was stressed out. My relationship wasn't fulfilling. I had slept with someone else. She didn't trust me anymore. I wasn't attracted to her and never had been.

I was lonely much of the time. I'd be at home working on my computer by myself, bored. What I wanted most was a fulfilling relationship.

I hated my job working at industrial sites. Having an apartment with no garage, I hung the rain-soaked and sulfur-dusted coveralls to dry in my entranceway, and the AC pushed the contaminants into my room. I was sick in bed for weeks. I had pneumonia.

There wasn't much money coming in. My living expenses were high. Rent was $1,600 per month, and I ate at restaurants most days. I certainly wasn't living profitably.

It was time for a change. I decided to leave the rat race. I quit my job and was so happy! I planned to go traveling in Mexico.

A couple of weeks later, I accepted an offer to continue doing office work as a contractor, so I was no longer an employee.

I vacated my apartment, putting my goods in storage at $80 per month. I ended my relationship.

I became a digital nomad, working from anywhere and traveling the world. I spent five months in the paradise of Mexico through the coldest Vancouver winter on record!

To regain my health, I swam every day and body boarded the waves. I weaned myself off restaurant meals, ate tropical fruit of all kinds and cut out dairy products. I felt stronger and healthier.

I defined my vision for the year and decided to do a weekly group call for free. During the first call, an attendee said, "I'm inspired to look at ways I can be more of service in the world." I felt amazing after the call. I was smiling widely as I walked along the beach.

Over time, I became known as the 'Position on Purpose Guy'. My friends introduced me to people I love working with who were looking for my services.

By going on this adventure in problem-solving, I gained clarity. I know what I'm here to do and I'm doing it. It feels wonderful and peaceful, mentoring a group of purposeful entrepreneurs because I'm walking daily in my purpose.

I also gained peace of mind, freedom, autonomy, excitement, adventure, and interesting new relationships. I lost a very comfortable and convenient life, and I lost the empty feeling! I learned many lessons along the way, and I share them with all members of Position On Purpose for free.

I believe you can achieve personal freedom by earning more than you spend, by doing something that you enjoy and care about.

I became clear by asking myself questions, going for long walks, being alone in nature, trying lots of things and measuring my enjoyment and excitement.

If you're in the same situation I was, unfulfilled in your life and work, I'd give you these tips to help change your life.

Answer these questions, and you'll set meaningful goals and likely enjoy your life more.

1. What do you want to experience?

2. How will you have to grow to have these experiences?

3. Once you have grown in those ways, how will you be able to contribute?

Do not fear. Your purpose will be something that you enjoy doing.

It's vital to become intimate with the infinite. Connect with your true self. Take a break from the everyday grind, get into nature and be in your element (which for me, is water). Once you're enjoying yourself in a peaceful state, start exploring your passions. What do you want to improve in the world or in people's lives?

Make a list of answers for each of these questions:

1. What do you love to do?

2. What are you great at?

3. What could other people pay you to teach them?

Look for overlaps in these three areas. When you find an intersection, this could be something you can teach online and start building a side income, which could grow over time. Eventually, you may be able to make a great living doing what you love, and no longer have to sell your time for money or do something that doesn't align with your core values.

Start changing lives and then figure out how to monetize. Want their success more than you want their money.

When you accept your purpose with excitement and joy, you will work with joy. Realize what you do is important and feel appreciated.

My mission is clear: create a world where work is joyful and comes from love. It feels peaceful and rewarding to be mentoring a group of clients who, like myself, are committed to evolving consciousness, helping them apply direct marketing principles to their soulful business and implement a simple business model that is leveraged, automated and scalable. We're growing together. I know I'm doing the right thing and I'm earning a growing side income doing what I love. Are you ready to come along on the journey?

What matters most to me is not how much money I earn, but that I am doing what I believe in and being true to myself.

Camille Roman

Camille Roman is a contemporary artist, certified reflexologist, and pranic healer, who has survived a life-threatening health scare and is completely immersed in helping others utilize holistic modalities for healing. Through her paintings, she inspires and uplifts by incorporating brilliant colors, texture and exaggerated perspective. Her work generates emotion and engages in a way that leaves her audience mentally and spiritually impacted for the better. She believes art is therapy for the mind, body and soul, and that artists can change the world. Through reflexology and pranic healing, she aids the body in its natural ability to heal itself.

Learn more about Camille:

Websites: www.camillefineart.com

www.yourjoyfulsoles.com

Instagram: www.instagram.com/camilleromanfineart

Chapter 3

Thank You,
Universe…Message Received!

By Camille Roman

Have you ever stopped dead in your tracks because you suddenly became aware of things happening around you? Not just ordinary things, but feeling as if God/the universe is manipulating people and events in your life like a game of chess? That is exactly what happened to me almost five years ago. My entire universe shifted.

I remember quite vividly a day at work in early March 2013, when I consciously noticed people coming into my life in ways I had always wanted. It was an odd feeling because normally I would be a shrinking violet. I was so blinded by a lack of self-worth that I didn't think I was important or interesting to others on a personal level. As a result, I allowed myself to blend into the wallpaper. At work, I was all business, because I was confident in my job and that was where I excelled. I didn't have to expose my private self. Close and caring friendships were starting to develop before my eyes, with little effort on my part. Various opportunities for learning health and healing modalities were presenting themselves to me, and I felt compelled to immerse myself in them. That evening I told my husband I believed something really big was going to happen. I described the things that had been occurring, not only that day, but for at least six months prior. I couldn't explain the feeling I was having, but I *knew* something significant was coming down the road… and it did. On March 26th, 2013, my life changed forever.

No one can fully prepare you for hearing the words, "Your tumor is malignant." In my case, I was pretty sure it was, but still… hearing those words out loud put me in a very surreal situation. I had been waiting for three days for that phone call. Now here I was, alone at work, tucked in a little alcove that wasn't very private, trying not to let passersby see tears streaming down my face. I know I had a full conversation with the specialist, but honestly… I don't remember much other than those frightening words. The discussion ended, I hung up the phone and sat there. So much was racing through my mind, but I couldn't hear. I couldn't see. I couldn't feel. It seemed like I sat there for an eternity. Finally, I mustered up the courage to make my way to the elevator. I had to speak with someone who wasn't my family. I couldn't even fathom how I was going to tell them, and I desperately needed to talk to someone, to say those words out loud so I could gain control of myself before facing them. I prayed so hard as that elevator made its way to my floor. In my mind, I kept saying, *Please God, please let my friend be at her desk.*

Fortunately, I found her, and we walked outside the building. As soon as we were far enough away I blurted out, "I have cancer. I just hung up with my doctor, and I have breast cancer! What am I going to do?" She stared at me with wide eyes. My poor friend didn't know what to do or say, except that she was so sorry. She hugged me as I was crying. I wept. I couldn't coherently form words. I only felt a deep, guttural instinct to scream. I wanted to scream so loudly it would ripple through time, but I couldn't. The screams remained inside. I felt as if I was in a fog, yet I knew I had to cry this desperation and fear out of me. Looking back, that was such a heavy load to dump on her unexpectedly, and I feel bad for dropping that bombshell on her. However, she didn't know how much she helped me at that moment in time by being the person on which I vomited all of my emotions.

Finally, I composed myself enough to return inside. We made our way to the elevator, and suddenly a resolve washed over me. It was like a wave of warm oil flowing down from my head slowly enveloping my entire body, and making its way down to my toes like a protective capsule. Instantly I made a decision. *This will not be the end of me*, I thought to myself. *This is nothing but a speed bump. I have a family I love, and I don't want to leave them. I will beat this. Whatever I have to do, I will do it*, I said to myself.

I left the office; the ride home was daunting. I called my husband to tell him I heard from the doctor, and we needed to talk. He gathered my son, and they were waiting for me when I arrived. I remember them sitting opposite one another in our dimly lit living room. The look on their faces was grim. Reaching deep inside me for courage, I took a deep breath and relayed the words from my doctor. It was as if someone sucked all the air out of the room. It pained me to see their expressions. I know it hurt them to hear those words, but I assured them it was going to be ok. They told me they loved me. My daughter lived out of state at the time, and I hated having to deliver a message like this over the phone, but it had to be done. Everyone was informed. Now the journey would begin.

I cannot convey how beautifully orchestrated the entrance of, or the stepping up of, the people in my life was who helped me through this journey. My family and co-workers rallied around me with much love and support. It was astounding and made it easier for me to focus on what I had to do.

The activities that followed occurred in a whirlwind. Though I researched various options, it was as if someone was guiding me on automatic pilot. There were times when it seemed I existed outside of my body, a spectator of my own life. Doctor appointments filled my days with information overload, and I went with my gut on the course of action. I wanted to be as holistic as possible to balance western medicine procedures. I dusted off my proverbial toolkit and started filling it with things that could help me.

First, I am an artist, and painting has always been my outlet to express joy, love, and creativity or work out anger, fear, and sadness. Throughout my health detour, I permitted myself the luxury of letting go. I painted from my soul and left all rules behind. Previously, I was afraid to waste supplies and time. I always had to make it right the first time. It had to be perfect, yet I never felt like my work quite measured up to that of 'real' artists. Facing this illness freed me. Threatened with the possibility of an early death, I took out all the stops! The vision of my life became crystal clear. I was a volcano of creative lava that flowed with reckless abandon! Through art I gave back to others confronting cancer, to encourage and uplift them. This was a positive result of the illness. The awakening. There are no accidents!

Second, I leaned into a vegetarian lifestyle and was feeling very healthy going into this battle. Thank goodness, because I believe wholeheartedly that if I wasn't in a healthier state, I might not have had the strength to survive what was to come.

Next, I learned a specific type of energy healing called pranic healing. I hadn't sought this out; it just kind of fell into my lap via an email feed. I read about it, it sounded interesting, so I went to my first meeting. I truly connected with the participants, and the instructor was intuitive and caring. I benefited by participating in weekly group meditation, and the energy work I performed on others and myself was rewarding. I definitely experienced a difference in my own body and psyche. I learned about the effects of emotions on the physical body. I intuitively knew about the impact of color on a person's mood and was utilizing it in my artwork. I studied how using various colored energies when performing pranic healing, could have an effect on clearing certain feelings or issues. This was very intriguing to me, and I used the technique on myself. As an artist, I am a great visualizer. During moments of fear or anxiety, I visualized something to help me through it. Like when I lay in that noisy, coffin-like tube for my MRI, I visualized little green and orange construction workers using jackhammers to break up my tumor in perfect concert with the unnerving pounding sounds of the exam. Had I not done that, I would have completely lost my mind being in that confined space for what seemed like forever! I discovered pranic breathing and physical exercises that are practiced before and after meditation, to keep the lymph and blood circulating, thereby reducing congestion. These routines played a major role in preparing my body for the upcoming surgery, recovery, and treatments that would follow.

I deliberately asked the doctors *not* to tell me the stage of my tumor. I didn't want to be influenced by a number. The emphasis society places on that designation totally messes with your psyche, and I was not going to have any of that! I didn't care about the stage because I wasn't going to allow that thought in my head. It was really difficult because one of the first things someone asks is, "So what stage are you?" I must have sounded like I was in denial because I said, "I don't know, and I don't want to know." Everyone is different physiologically, and even though we are all human, there is *no* one-stop cure for any disease. I may be blood type O+, but you know what? Some other O+ person isn't the same as me. There are differences in our individual make-ups so *never* get caught up in 'the number'. Only I could make the difference in living or dying. Attitude wins the game or loses it! If I insisted on staying stuck in my head listening to all the chatter I made sure it was good, positive, inspiring stuff!

The time span between my surgery and the start of my chemo was crucial to my health. I started exercising in the recovery room as soon as I was conscious enough to move my wrists, arms, feet. I exercised in my bed throughout the day and night at the hospital. Lord knows sleeping in the hospital is impossible because nurses wake you up every twenty minutes to ask you if you are ok, even if it is 2 am! May as well utilize the wake time doing something useful, right? I also meditated several times a day. When released, I continued those practices and made sure I was eating as much 'live food' as possible in the forms of juices, parboiled soups and drinking lots of pure water. Chemo was next on the list, and I needed to get ready for the fight!

Chemotherapy, whoa! I was so allergic to what they gave me that I had to be drugged with Benadryl. Fortunately, I slept through most of it. I was even allergic to the medicine they prescribed to help with my bones. I returned home the first day, and my son asked if I was ok. I responded, "Yea, why?" Evidently, I had a target-like rash forming from the tip of my nose, steadily spreading to my neck. I made it through the sessions, but the last four nearly killed me. My bones hurt so badly that I just prayed and painted my way through it. My daughter returned home and was my angel with the care she gave me.

Vanity! One of the hardest things was losing my hair.... more so than losing my breast. Weird, I know, but true. I recall telling my doctor at the infamous two weeks target date, "I know you said my hair would fall at two weeks out, but look how strong it is! I think I will be fine." No kidding, within two days my hair starting falling out everywhere. That unnerved me; I knew it was time to cut it. My family gathered, and my future daughter-in-law and son lovingly cut it. My son's eyes filled with tears because it was so painful for him to watch. In solidarity, my husband and grandson cut off their hair too. God love them!

I returned to work wearing a wig, but couldn't stand how hot it was! So I started wearing all kinds of hats, and kept myself perky and uplifted for my own psyche. Before I knew it, people I never spoke with previously told me how cute, or inspiring I was to them. It hadn't occurred to me about the effect I might have on others. I never thought anyone cared about what I had to say or even noticed me. Part of how I got into this health situation was not having enough self-love, and now I was inspiring people. That touched my soul, and I realized people watch us even if we don't know it. We can impact others positively or negatively without being conscious of it because we are so wrapped up in our own little minds. This was a game-changer for me. I started *knowing* that I make a difference. If I could make *me* better, my example could positively guide those around me.

For instance, empowerment! During radiation, I empathically protested against the lotions provided to me by the hospital because they were filled with parabens and petroleum! I couldn't believe they gave me the same harmful chemicals that helped cause the cancer I was trying to fight! Much to my doctor's dismay, I selected my own products, and the staff was astonished at how healthy my skin remained during treatments. I felt like a conqueror of big pharma by winning that battle with the doctor!

This journey has been amazing. If you were to ask anyone who knew me before and after my brush with mortality, I am certain most people would say I am a different person. One who has confidence, a voice, and has skyrocketed in her ability to learn and teach others. I understand now that the old version of me, and the experience of my illness, were stepping-stones to the role I'm meant to play in the universe. There is a divine plan for me, whether I want to believe it or not, whether I am conscious of it or not. Message received! Each encounter brings me closer to my destiny. I look forward to the path ahead of me, and I am thankful because each day of life is a gift of love!

Cyndi Robinson Sanders

Cyndi Robinson Sanders is an expansion coach who guides clients in pursuit of their best life dreams. Studying with many transformational leaders and authors allows her to expand her own life continuously. A key tenet of her coaching are the laws of the universe.

Cyndi's passion for training, mentoring and coaching was born in her early career with large and small businesses. She is married and loves traveling the world from her home in the US Pacific Northwest. Cyndi was greatly inspired by her father Howard (a lifelong Boy Scout professional) to learn the ability to dream and be in service to others.

Learn more about Cyndi:

Email: Cyndi@BestLifeDreams.com

Instagram: www.instagram.com/2ChicksonFire

Website: http://cyndisanders.com/

Chapter 4

Baggage, I Don't Need Any Stinkin' Baggage!

By Cyndi Robinson Sanders

When I was twenty-three, I stopped counting the number of times I had moved. My dad's career meant we moved every time he changed positions within the same company. As an adult, moving is an inconvenience. As a very sensitive child that always felt different, it was as if my whole world was falling apart. The feeling that I would never have a special friend of my own began to rise within me. I learned early on to stuff my feelings into bags and store them away.

Decades ago, I could see things coming true that I thought about, dreamed of, wished for and worried about. I knew deep inside me from an early age that I 'saw' things differently than my sisters and the kids in the neighborhood. It appeared to me that everyone had their own special friend, everyone except me.

I have many stories of manifestations followed quickly by heartache as I grew up. One day, I realized that I had always pushed away or delayed love. I had observed many relationships sour around me. I tiptoed into the world of dating at thirty realizing by fearing heartache, I could never experience the opposite – joy. My first 'date' manifested a few months later. My first sexual experience was one of those highs, followed by being completely ignored. I mucked around using a string of men to make me feel good about myself. I dreamed of my soulmate appearing, but at the same time, I didn't believe that I deserved it.

When I met and quickly married my first husband, I knew I had manifested that dream guy from my childhood; the rainy day catalog cut-out collages of my future. He looked deep into my eyes and 'saw me'. He told me things he saw in me that I had never told anyone in the world. We talked on the phone on a regular basis for professional reasons but eventually decided to meet in person. We were married ten days later!

Alas, our first few months of married life were not easy. I had quit my two jobs and moved to the other end of the state where he lived. I started to worry a lot about the cultural differences between us, how quickly we had married without a 'getting to know each other period' and our tight financial situation. Previous employers called, begging me to come back, and we decided I would go to help make ends meet.

We conceived a child on a weekend trip together, but that pregnancy developed issues early on, and the baby did not make it to term. I quickly perceived that the spark I had seen in his eyes when we married was only appearing when he spoke of a specific female client.

I discovered a plane ticket for that same woman – for when I would be away working – in his closet. All I could think of was that I had manifested a man who was not loyal to me. I packed up my clothing, a few prized possessions, and moved within a couple weeks of that discovery before she came to visit. Unable or unwilling to deal with my perception – either way – all I could think about was that my greatest fear had come true. My special someone had never been mine.

Alas, in hindsight, I was a powerful manifester who attracted him then pushed him away in so many ways. We ultimately filed for divorce a couple years later when I was ready to pull my next act of running away and move across the country.

I had become used to the nomadic way of life. I powerfully manifested things I wanted and feared. When the negative experiences, sad times, or broken hearts came around, I would run away. I later would call this the times of my life when I 'pulled a geographic'.

Just before the turn of the century, I finally braved making some good female friends. I joined an organization that formed small groups to study for six months at a time on specific transformational topics, always on relationships. I was called upon to lead a writing group to create a program to prepare women for a long-term, committed relationship. I wanted that dream badly, so I leaned fully into that project.

Over the next year, self-discovery was a big part of my life. I did the work while creating the program. I did the work again as a student in one of the first group classes offered. I asked for and received mentors living the marriages I could see in my visions. I often repeated the statement 'When I get around to buying a house, I will meet the right man for me and he'll have a house'. I was lucky enough to have a dream job that kept me on the go traveling weekly and meeting many men.

For eighteen months prior to the horrific 9/11 tragedies, I had traveled out of one of those fated airports every Monday. I had literally just been assigned locally. It struck me hard that I didn't have a special man of my own that cared enough about me to check on me. I sat there alone watching the events of that day unfold.

I set out on a plan to move again. This time, however, I was not running away from something, I was running *toward* something. I decluttered, donated, and gave away my unwanted possessions. I spent those months working near home downsizing. I did so with some good friends. I never again worried about making friends. I had finally mastered making friends when I wanted, after a lifetime of feeling as if it was impossible.

I knew in my heart I wanted to live closer to my aging parents on the opposite coast, so I started traveling for work again. I visited my parents who lived with my youngest sister and her family. I absolutely loved the area and I bought a condo that weekend! I traveled across the country to move my belongings to my first ever 'home'. One of the gals from the women's group even drove with me to my new home to settle me in and make sure I kept dreaming every mile along the way to my new life.

This time dating was different. I was looking forward to a new way of meeting people. I had 'done the work' over the previous three years. I knew who I was, and what I needed in a relationship. I had a vision of what I wanted the relationship to be. I had a list of qualities and characteristics he would possess. I had a new home and the mortgage to go with it. At forty-three, I felt like I had arrived at adulthood.

Those mentors I mentioned before? One thing they often repeated was that when I finally felt completely ok living with myself without a man, he would arrive. I remembered their wisdom clearly. It mirrored one of my favorite movie lines. In *Somewhere in Time,* the main female character says to a man that seems to be pursuing her: "Is it you?" I even asked myself when I bought the washer and dryer, *Would this be the set my future husband would buy if he were with me?*

I was sitting in my living room the day I realized my life felt perfect. I had just been sent on a series of international assignments, had flown business class, and stayed in five-star hotels – all since buying my condo. The only thing that might have to change when 'he' arrived was the girly floral wallpaper in the hall. I laughed out loud and basked in the appreciation of what I had created for myself.

Bam. Within six weeks of living my perfect life, I 'met' him online. For once, he was local and had just moved from an area close to where I lived previously. The conversations in email and on the phone flowed easily. It felt like he was the one! We scheduled a lunch date. Then *bam...* he disappeared. I chalked it off to 'almost' and kept true to my dating plan, bolstered with the knowledge I had done years of work and understood what I needed.

Six weeks later, I was going through and canceling unnecessary services after a layoff. I ran across his name and emailed to warn him I might not be able to reach him after I canceled the service. He wrote back acknowledging he had flaked on lunch and suggested dinner the following Friday. I can see now I did not trust that he would follow through, so I arranged a date for earlier that day. He showed up!

About halfway through the dinner, he shared that earlier that day he had bought a house. Chills ran up my spine. He liked everything I had planned, and we laughed a lot. He was a gentleman, and didn't suggest any dalliance after dinner and asked if he could call again. I went home wondering, *is he the one,* given I what I had said over and over to my girlfriends about meeting a man when I bought a house.

41

I reviewed the emails we had swapped weeks before, and I noticed that in the first email I had asked him what he considered to be the perfect date. I had forgotten his reply and glowed as I read that I had executed his plan. I'll skip ahead after sharing one more thing; remember the washer & dryer? When he saw it for the first time in my condo he exclaimed, "I bought that same exact set at my last house in California!"

My bubble burst...but not right away. I waited a bit longer this time to marry – eleven months! We married on an idyllic day on the coast. Just as I had envisioned it. We worked through getting to know each other, through financial strains and stressful jobs. We saved three years to have a first-class three-week honeymoon in Europe. I had been able to live the life of my dreams, volunteering, learning, enjoying time with him and 'me time' without him while he worked out of state four days a week. We argued a little, but nothing that would involve us seeking couples counseling. I did seek individual counseling. After a few sessions, I ended it feeling I already knew how to deal with my issues.

Then my father died, and our communication issues started to accelerate. Rather than seek outside help, I once again stuffed my feelings into bags. Several months later my husband's uncle died. I could write several chapters about the angst that grew rapidly over the next two years.

I ended up moving and living out of a suitcase while assisting my in-laws. The only time I got home was to have a root canal. My husband was the breadwinner in the family and felt his weekends were for fun. I certainly did not feel like I had any support from him. All I really wanted to do was run away.

My 'work', while single, didn't involve planning this stage of a marriage. As the wife of an only child, I certainly should have anticipated this role prior to marriage. I was no longer living the dream and was pissed as hell about it. I spent money gambling because liquor is often available cheaply in casinos. The days my husband was in town I was angry he could not 'see me' deteriorating and crumbling before his eyes. When I asked for help from him and did not get what I wanted, how and when I wanted it, I would respond mean and viciously.

The baggage I brought to marriage crash-landed. I never felt enough, I never felt special, that first failed marriage, and so many more pounds of crap. I was able to cram most of feelings and fears back in their cases and padlock them.

My drinking continued, until one morning I woke up parked behind the bank. The bank was eight miles from home, an equal distance from a bar I had 'closed'. Over the next few days, I stopped drinking and experienced the shakes of withdrawals. My husband didn't notice.

I delayed rehab to honor my promise to take care of my mom after post-surgery the following week. My husband expressed anger that I would not be home on weekends. I sat in the car at the ocean screaming, "Who the f*c* did I marry?" at the top of my lungs.

Once Mom had recovered, I attempted to find a rehab facility. My insurance would not pay for it because I had 'successfully' not drank for over twenty-one days on my own. I tried to communicate clearly to my husband that rehab was important. I felt that opening and discarding all that baggage required focus.

During the same week I was rejected for rehab, my husband broke our marriage vows by having a fling with a coworker. He didn't wait to tell me until we got home, he told me while I was driving! I remember screeching off the highway in his prized Cadillac. I parked it in the middle of a main road, tossed the keys in the shrubs and ran behind a building screaming, "How did I manifest this?" I was in a full-blown breakdown. It was easy to see in hindsight that I was not being my best self. I had withheld a lot; hid things and lied, but I was never unfaithful to him, not physically at least. I had brought the breakdown upon myself.

This time I chose not to run away. I did not seek out advice columns, online groups or the like. My previous work as a single woman to 'manifest' the right man for me proved my husband was that man. It allowed me to understand that he is a good man. My addiction, then sobriety, had changed the dynamics of our marriage but it had not changed who he was.

I took my time. I chose to trust the previous work I had done. I remembered that marriage is not an event, rather it is a journey. I continued to 'do the work' to understand myself. We evaluated counselors until we found the right match for both joint and individual sessions. They gave us a roadmap to healing. I trusted we both wanted to make our marriage last.

Now five years later, I do not regret staying or not asking him to leave. Is our marriage easy? No, but it is worth the journey. Each month we experience a high or a low, a twist or a turn. I get to celebrate the wins and the journey with a man I know, deep inside, *does* love me and I know he is my special one. He proves it day after day demonstrating I am his special one. We continue to do the work together.

David Phillips

David Phillips is the founder and president of Energetic Awakenings in Cleveland, OH. He is a leader in mind, body, and spiritual healing. David works with clients to identify roots causes that prevent them from being their authentic self and to take actions to achieve personal transformation. His main goal is to help each client 'Live Life Fully'. In his private practice, David works with individuals, couples, and groups.

He is also a workshop leader and group facilitator for many organizations dealing with challenging topics such as racism, LGBTQ cultural competency, leadership, and change. David holds his Master of Education from Cleveland State University with a focus on adult learning and development. He is a certified Core Energetics practitioner, reiki master, and certified coach.

Learn more about David:

Website: www.energeticawakenings.com

Facebook: https://www.facebook.com/energeticawakenings/

LinkedIn: https://www.linkedin.com/in/d4phillips/

Chapter 5

Coming Out of the Closet to Live Life Fully!

By David Phillips

You might say that grief was the key that unlocked the door to my transformation, but that sounds a little too neat, a bit too clean. Really, the transformation began when I decided that I deserved to be happy – which meant I had to leave a sixteen-year relationship with a man who I really loved. I had to learn to be completely authentic.

Let's take a step back. Growing up in West Virginia, the youngest of two, I was deep in the closet. In that world, it was not ok to be gay – in fact – it was potentially dangerous. My parents were divorced when I was two, and I didn't have much of a relationship with my father. Most of my best friends were girls. I was the person who did whatever I needed to do to prove myself the best. I was class president, co-drum captain, student council representative, and in the honor society. I did all those things to prove my self-worth, to prove I was ok, all the time hiding a part of me. Not allowing myself to be authentic was very exhausting.

When I got to college, I began to slowly test the waters. I remember riding home one weekend with my friend Crystal. I was trying to tell her I was gay in a very indirect way. I began telling her about a sociology paper I had written that was about different kinds of people. I was gauging her response to gay people. All of a sudden, she grabbed my arm and said, "Honey, are you trying to tell me something? Cause I love you, and I will love you regardless." I was so moved; I began to cry. Crystal was awesome. She stood by my side throughout college, always assuring me I was ok, just being me. I experienced many similar situations with others. Each gift of unexpected unconditional love and acceptance took me by surprise. I truly believed that people would not understand or accept me. This is the story that I carried with me for almost forty years. I feel blessed that many of my closest friends embraced me and loved me as I shared with them the part of me I had been struggling to keep secret. However, I still could not reveal my true self to my family.

After college, I moved to Ohio. I felt I had to move away to have the freedom to be me. I was working in a hotel, and I met Kevin. Over time, I fell in love and was in a relationship with him for sixteen years. We shared many great times and truly loved each other. As time passed, I became increasingly unhappy. I still felt a deep love for Kevin, and although we worked to stay together, I eventually made the agonizing decision to end our relationship. It took me three years to turn this decision into a realization.

As I was concluding my time with Kevin, it became obvious that I had to finally reveal my full self to my mom and sister. I knew that ending my relationship with Kevin would put me on an emotional roller coaster. It would not make sense to my family that I was that upset over my 'roommate' moving out. I now realize that somewhere deep inside, I longed for their understanding and support. So on December 23rd, 2010, I decided to have the conversation with my mom and sister. I was terrified. My heart was racing. I didn't know the right words. I could not even use the word 'gay'. Finally, I explained that Kevin was to me, what my sister's husband was to her. A flood of tears exploded among the three of us! "You had to know," I eventually said to my sister. "I hoped and prayed I was wrong," she said. I was afraid my mom and sister would abandon me; kick me out of the family. To my surprise and relief, they did not! Today, they continue to believe that being gay is morally wrong and I am headed to hell. I fear this will always be a barrier in our relationship. Nevertheless, I know they will always love me.

The fact that they didn't kick me out of the family once the truth came out was a huge weight off my shoulders. Three months later, on St. Patrick's Day, I finally told Kevin that the relationship was over; I could not go on like this. It was very difficult for both of us. So many tears, so much heartache, yet I knew it had to be done. It genuinely hurt in the depths of my heart and soul. I was scared, and I didn't know what to do with myself. I quickly decided to pull up my bootstraps and move on. I made the decision, it was what I wanted, but I still wondered why I felt so sad.

My friends were urging me to seek professional counseling. I kept insisting that I was fine, but they wouldn't quit – and they were right. I found an LGBT-friendly therapist. At the same time, I began classes with Maia Beatty on *Powerful Presence*. I went to therapy at 3:00 pm and then to Maia's class at 5:00 pm. Maia assigned homework that included taking action in our lives. Suddenly, I could see things actually happening. I was beginning to make changes. The work with Maia was my first step toward positive transformation.

I felt the desire to continue to grow as a gay man, so I decided to attend a spiritual retreat. This thought was foreign to me. Typically, I only believed in what I could see with my own eyes and hear with my ears. My former partner Kevin and some of *his* friends were the ones interested in spiritual practices and energy work like Reiki. I was the skeptic. To me, it had all sounded like BS. Yet, I knew I needed to continue my journey, so I was willing to attempt a retreat.

I decided to go to a gay men's retreat in the Poconos that was focused on joy and happiness.

I told one of my best friends, Patty, about my plans. She was excited for me and suggested, "Before you go, let my sister do some energy work with you. It will help you be more open and receptive at the retreat." Remember, I was a skeptic, and my immediate thought was BS. Patty would not let go of the idea, so I finally agreed. Her sister, Teri, lives in Arizona and was going to do the work remotely... Right, more BS... or so I thought.

Teri called me the night before the retreat. She asked me to lie on the ground in a place where I felt safe. She began her work. I remember lying there thinking, *This is totally stupid.* She eventually said, "There is a block in your abdomen. Can you give it permission to release?" "Sure," I told her, still doubting. Suddenly there was a jolt that went through my whole body. "Oh shit!" I said. "This is *real!*" She asked if I was ok and said, "That was really big! What do you mean 'it's real'?" I told her I would explain later and to finish what she was doing. When she finished the treatment, I confessed that I had never believed in energy work. "Now you get it?" she asked. I told her I really didn't, but at least now I believed it was real.

The next day, I went to the retreat with twelve other gay men. I started out like a scared kid on his first day of school. Eventually, I settled in, and it was an incredible experience. I began to realize I was shut down. I allowed myself to begin to feel the pain. I explored allowing other men to support me. I had never been surrounded by a group of men with such compassion, support, and care. It was incredible! At the retreat, I met Andrew, who told me about another retreat called Living Full Out. "You should go," he said. "It will change your life!" It turned out he was right, in more ways than I could have imagined.

I registered for the retreat at Easton Mountain and was contacted by John, one of the facilitators, to conduct an interview. He explained that the work focused on expressing emotions and healing wounds. I felt I needed to mourn the ending of my relationship so, it sounded perfect! I went with an open mind. When it was my turn for individual work, one of the facilitators, Richard, was working on my abdomen. He told me I had emotions stuck inside. I was lying on the ground while he deeply massaged my abdomen. The other facilitator, John, held my head gently. He asked me to place my legs against a mattress and just press so I could get some energy into my legs. The mattress was being held up by eight men. I was pressing against it, and nothing was happening. "It's hard for you to let go, isn't it?" John said. "You keep things inside as a way of protecting yourself, right?" I nodded yes. He asked one of the guys to say something to me. I heard a female voice say, "David, this is your mother. We're praying for you." I was unexpectedly enraged and not only began pushing on the mattress but knocked eight men on their asses! When it was over, I didn't understand what had happened, but I felt like something had been taken away; I felt lighter. *Whatever this was*, I thought, *I want more*. I signed up to attend the same retreat a couple of months later and had another amazing, cathartic experience.

I was intrigued by what was possible during these retreats. I wanted to learn how to hold that space for others. I asked Richard about his training and how he had become so skilled at unlocking the emotions locked in the body. He led me to the Institute of Core Energetics in New York City, where I attended an introductory class. During that weekend, I had more amazing experiences. I spoke to the director about moving forward and learned that no one in my area was doing that kind of work, so I'd have to commute for training. I did the commute for five years. I would fly in for classes on a Wednesday or Thursday and then fly back to Cleveland on the following Monday or Tuesday. I did this at least five times each year.

During these five years, the healing continued. Every time I would go to a weekend class, I would uncover more and more of the emotions and feelings I had been hiding. I would discover images and stories that I believed to be true and found out that they simply were not. Some of my fables included: my family hates me because I am gay, all straight men hate me because I am gay, I am not good enough or lovable because I am gay. These are difficult themes to deal with when you *really* are gay. I am grateful that there have been many people and lots of moments that have helped me to realize the truth.

Let's start with my family. My mom and my sister *really* love me a lot. They love me so much that they want what is best for me. They still have an entrenched belief system that says being gay is morally wrong and I am headed to hell. Although I struggle with their acceptance, I know they *truly* love me. I had always been afraid to tell my dad that I was gay. My story was that he would reject me and say he didn't want a fag for a son. When I finally had the conversation with him in my third year of Core Energetics training, he said, "Son, I have known for a long time, and there is nothing more that I want than a relationship with my boy." That was such a healing moment. Another weight had been lifted off my body. I am happy to say after twenty years of not visiting my dad I recently visited him in his home and had an incredible time.

Let's move on to straight men. Straight men don't actually hate me because I am gay. Two of my greatest teachers are Doug and Tony. Doug was a former boss who sincerely accepts me, just as I am. When I told him that I ended my relationship with Kevin, he stopped, took a deep breath, tears rolled down his face, and he said, "Are you really ok? You have been with Kevin longer than I have been married." This made me feel seen, held and loved at that moment. Tony is a retired Air Force colonel who was also a student in my Core Energetics class. Initially, I was so intimidated by this man. Over the past six years, he has grown to be my brother. He held my hand as I told my dad I was gay. We have cried, laughed, and celebrated life. Finally, the ManKind Project has helped me create a network of men who show me love and compassion. These men are amazing! Aho!

My belief that I am not lovable or good enough is consistently challenged by an amazing group of friends; many of whom I consider my chosen family. They make it hard to believe I am not lovable. I am enormously blessed with a large circle of amazing people who give me complete acceptance and love. Some are more 'in my face' than others, but I am grateful when Karla, Clare, Pat, Wendy, Patty, Doug, Carol, Tony, Tristan, Maia, Paula, Chris (the list goes on) get 'in my face' and remind me that I am a good man, and I *deserve* love.

Now, the journey continues! I learn to love myself more every day. I am blessed that through this process, I have successfully established a private practice where I am honored to hold space and help people heal. This work is powerful and provides healing for those who are willing to take the journey.

Things that I have learned that I will leave with you to help support you:

- Healing is a journey, not a destination.

- Be your authentic self; it might be scary, but it's easier.

- Love yourself, love yourself, love yourself.

- Face your fears; they are only false expectations appearing real.

- Don't let others judge your path: they have not traveled in your shoes.

- Embrace your full self - mind, body, spirit, will, and emotions.

- Look at yourself in the mirror every day; look deep inside. Tell yourself that you matter and that you are lovable.

- Ask for support; it is braver and takes more courage to ask for support than to do it alone.

- Vulnerability and genuine connection create long-lasting friendships and relationships.

- The key to unlocking yourself is most likely hidden within your own body: do the work to find it so you can live life fully!

Donna Marie Laino

Donna Marie Laino knew she wanted to be a nurse when she was three years old. With a passion to empower people to become more, she became a holistic practitioner, life coach, neuro-linguistic practitioner and certified clinical aromatherapist.

As a graduate of PBS chef Christina Pirello's School of Natural Cooking and Integrative Health Studies, she helps people create balance in their life by utilizing holistic modalities and teaching people healthy ways to cook and eat.

Using the healing power of humor, she is a certified laughter leader and clown and is highlighted in the documentary film, The Real Patch Adams. She enjoys speaking, writing, and ballroom dancing.

Learn more about Donna Marie:

Websites: www.donnamarielaino.com

http://www.ArticlesByDonnaMarie.com

Email: info@DonnaMarieLaino.com

Chapter 6

From Zero to Hero

By Donna Marie Laino

'Shifts Happen.'

That is the first thing I saw when I walked into the farmhouse of Patch Adam's Gesundheit! Institute in the summer of 1997. I had just been laid-off as a nurse in the role of director of community health education and three months out from getting my graduate degree from La Salle University.

As I was finishing my thesis, I remember lying in the tub overwhelmed and crying about the struggles of my life. My husband had tried to calm me down and said that I could not have it all: house, family, and a career. I told him that I *could* and was *determined* to prove it.

I successfully finished what the dean called a doctoral level thesis, after losing 10,000 bits of inputted data by mistake, bought a house and figured out how to adopt two children from Thailand without an agency doing the behind the scenes work. I was told it was impossible to do, but I found a way. All I had to do was to decide.

Make the decision; that was the first step.

Somehow, I easily found an agency to do the home study, and because I was determined to adopt, I found out what to do, jumped all the hurdles of endless problem solving, and learned when to speak to foreign adoption officers who were twelve hours ahead of my time zone. Not only did I learn to problem-solve, but I also became a student learning how to master *critical thinking*.

These critical thinking skills sharpened my mind, kept me focused on the goal and I was able to adopt a Thai child not once, but twice; my daughters Nune and Orrawan.

Little did I know that this would set me up to attract what I needed next along my journey. I am a believer in the saying, '*When the student is ready, the teacher will appear*'.

I met Bill Gove and Steve Siebold while at the airline ticket counter trying to get home to Philadelphia after two flights left me stranded on the West Coast. I caught Bill's attention as I was wearing a chicken hat, one of many from my clown chest. I recognized who he was immediately, as I had seen him speak on stage two times as well as Steve. Bill Gove (*the father of public speaking*), Steve and I became friends, and by 'coincidence', I ended up on their flight on my way home.

After studying and mentoring with Bill and Steve, one day I got a phone call from Cary Glickstein, my upline Diamond in Nikken, the MLM health and wellness Japanese company. He asked me if I wanted to participate in a pilot program that none other than Steve Siebold was going to form. I said yes without even blinking. It was called the Tiger Program, and soon after that, I was on a call with Steve to find out the details. Several of my Philadelphia crossline friends were also in the group, and we formed an alliance, cheering for and supporting each other.

Steve told us it would not be easy and the requirements were rather rigorous. If you failed to meet the weekly requirements, you'd have to pay $50 to a charity and face the group during a weekly call. I agreed to the ten-week program where I had to call and make contact with fifty people per week, keep daily logs and fax them into the Gove-Siebold office by the designated date and time each week.

I made the decision that failure was not an option.

We had our prep call, I made my lists, gathered phone numbers and the materials I needed to make the journey.

Ready, set, go.

Then it happened. I did not realize that I was going to have a visceral reaction. I was calling people to invite them to schedule a meeting with me to discuss the wellness products that Nikken offered. The products could sell themselves. However, I needed to deliver a convincing speech in a short period of time on the phone to pique their interest. I was not prepared for what was about to happen.

I was going to throw up.

With my hand on the phone and my feet pointed to run into the bathroom, I had to make a quick decision on what to do.

Failure is not an option, I told myself.

With the saliva building up in my mouth, I quickly dialed Steve's number, and he answered the phone. His words were quick and simple:

"Donna, go throw up and come back and pick up the phone."

I had hit the wall and failure was not an option.

I did exactly what my mentor told me to do, and I made my fifty calls despite being physically ill. As the first deadline approached, I placed the total number of appointments I made in a circle at the top of the page.

Zero.

Several weeks went by with 'Zero' written on top of the page. I met the requirements each week, but I could not make appointments. I thought I was way out of my league; I did not go to nursing school for this. I was proud that I met the requirements each week and did not drop out or have to pay the fine. I watched others in the Tiger Program fail to make the commitment, so they paid the money to the charity, and some eventually dropped out.

To help cheer me on, my kids made signs for me that centered around their mom being a 'tiger'. They gave me tiger pictures that they drew along with their tiger animals, which I placed around me on my desk where I made the calls. This encouragement and the mental toughness mentoring I received from Steve Siebold got me thinking I was the next 'Italian Stallion' here in my hometown of Philadelphia. It was at that point that I took on the Rocky Balboa image of toughness.

I began to play the Rocky theme song both on the stereo and in my head before sitting down to make my fifty plus calls. As no answers did not count, I had to make more than fifty calls to meet the requirements each week. It was not an easy task. Soon after that, numbers started to appear in the circle at the top of my data sheets, and my tiger cub peers were cheering for me. I saw myself as the boxer, much like my grandfather Anthony Maurelli in his youth as Tommy Russell, the lightweight fighter.

In the kitchen, I prepared myself with the music on, and I would do a sparring routine with imaginary gloves on, fighting the demons of cold calling as they came up and knocked out any self-esteem issues I had of not being good enough to do the job. Many times, I had tears in my eyes, and as the *Eye of the Tiger* song progressed, they would stream down my cheeks onto the floor during my preparation.

In order to grow through it, I had to go through it.

The words of the song became my mantra, and I used guided imagery to visualize myself in each one of the stanzas. *'Rising up, back on the street, did my time, took my chances. Went the distance now I'm back on my feet... with the will to survive, you must fight just to keep them alive.'*

I fought all those things that held me back and this kept me where I was. I was secretly imploding every time I allowed myself to stay within my comfort zone. *There is no growth there, only safety.*

I made a transition with this fighting song:

I became the song.

I became the words.

I became the tiger!

I felt it in me, the tiger. I *was* the tiger. I looked in the mirror on my desk before I picked up the phone and I would say, "I am the tiger," out loud. I would even roar for added effect.

Soon, double-digit numbers appeared in the circle at the top of my data sheets. I was confident and reassured. There was no stopping me. I had 'the will to survive'. I was alive. I was the 'Tiger'.

I picked up the phone one day; it was Steve Siebold. The Tiger Pilot Program had finished, and he asked me if I was going to Toronto for the Nikken Team Diamond conference. I told him yes. He and Bill Gove were presenting the Tiger Program on stage

Saturday morning. Steve said that I had won the 'Most Achieved Tiger Award' and that he and Bill would be presenting it to me on stage after he told my story.

I was speechless.

Tears streamed down my face, and I began to sob. My whole life flashed before me – the life of not being good enough, feeling small, climbing into the abyss, the speech problems, being born with a facial deformity, never feeling pretty because of scars, and always wondering if I made a difference. I just never felt like I was enough. Now I would be taking my victory lap, having broken through the terror barrier, achieving on average, twenty-one appointments per week.

My children helped me make a tiger tail, and we stuffed it after finding tiger material at the fabric store. I wore everything possible that I could find that had a tiger print including a safari hat and pants. I pinned toy tiger animals on my blazer, and I walked around as the 'Tiger' at the conference.

Steve met me early that Saturday morning in the large ballroom before the event had begun. As he told me he was going to tell my story then hand me the microphone at the bottom of the stage, I thought to myself; *There is no way I am going to receive the tiger award on the floor. I will be on stage to get this award!*

Like the Tiger Program, I did not know how I was going to do it; I just knew it would be so. I saw myself on stage with Bill and Steve.

As Steve introduced the Tiger Pilot Program, participants, requirements, data and how mental toughness was the thread that was woven into the success pattern of the program, I heard my story being told on stage. Steve is a great storyteller and professional speaker, and I could not believe it was *my story* he was telling. I heard my 'cue' and stood up at the base of the platform on the floor as Steve handed me the microphone.

As I began to tell my story over the loud clapping, someone yelled, "Stand up!" The crowd wanted to see me! I turned and as Steve lifted me up; the audience of over three thousand people saw my tiger tail and began to laugh.

I was so excited to tell my version of the story, my passion, my 'will to survive,' that I transformed into the 'Tiger' on stage.

My one minute of allotted speaking time went into three minutes, and Steve had to take the microphone from my hands.

I felt the victory that came with thousands of people clapping and cheering in a standing ovation in the giant ballroom. I felt powerful and accomplished.

After the mental toughness session had ended and Bill and Steve got off the stage, there was a break before the next speaker, which was Bob Proctor. A long line formed in front of me of people wanting to talk with me. I did not know any of them. Some had tears in their eyes as they spoke of similar feelings of being held back at the threshold of the terror barrier, afraid and unable to pass through. Some hugged me so tight I could not breathe. Words of congratulations and well-wishing took up the entire break time so much so that I had to bring the line to the back of the room as Bob Proctor had already begun speaking.

I touched so many people's lives that day. Steve said that my story would be told around the world because of the recording that was made of the conference. I felt very full.

At the conference, people continued to see me with the tigers pinned all over me and stopped me to talk – even in the bathroom. I got phone calls from a leader in London wanting me to speak to his group, and from others around the country wanting me to do the same. I did not realize how impactful my story was until I went to a Bob Proctor Life Success facilitator's workshop and sat down at a table. The gentleman across from me saw me and my name tag and said, "I knew you would be here." The woman seated to my right began to speak to me and tears filled up in her eyes. She was from England and had heard my story and seen me on stage. When she went home to England, she told her nine-year-old son the story of my fright, breakthrough, courage, and triumph. Indeed, my experience had traveled across the globe and became a viral story of encouragement. My words gave this boy courage.

She talked about how my story affected her personally and gave her hope. Tears filled my eyes when she said she never dreamed she would actually meet me, but here I was sitting right next to her.

She had manifested *me*!

I did not realize what an impact my story had on people and to what lengths it would travel. In fact, I will never truly know.

Because of my shifting, I felt powerful, free and most importantly, in my power. I had proof that I could achieve my goals and manifest what I want.

I went from zero to hero.

We bring our life events to every challenge, whether they are good or bad. Each event impacts us differently. In order to prevent breakdowns, here are some tips I recommend to achieve breakthroughs:

- Set goals.

- Make a decision and commitment.

- Take action.

- Get a mentor and accountability coach.

- Use mental toughness and critical thinking skills.

Remember this: there is a *tiger* in all of us. Go the distance, get the guts, and get the glory!

Dorci Hill

Dorci Hill is known as the 'realistic' wellness lifestyle expert because she refuses to live in a world without cheesecake! She works with her clients to determine their vision of a healthy lifestyle. She then develops simple steps and micro habits to make this lifestyle a reality.

Dorci has lived a healthy, medication/antibiotic free lifestyle for over fifteen years; her passion is empowering clients with the tools to lasting health. She has an Associates of Applied Arts and a B.S in Biology/Chemistry. Dorci is a coach, 2-time best-selling author, speaker, and certified facilitator of the healing dance therapy - ChakradanceTM,

Learn more about Dorci:

Website: www.dorcihillglobal.com

Email: dorci@dorcihillglobal.com

Facebook: www.facebook.com/dorcihillglobalwellness

Chapter 7

Health with Benefits

By Dorci Hill

Nothing ever seems to happen in the daylight. It's always evening or early morning. This was no different. As I lay there in the quiet, so many thoughts ran through my mind. Twelve months, two hospital visits, and three prescriptions. All by the age of thirty. Not exactly the scenario I was hoping for when I left my twenties behind.

An aortic aneurysm, blockage, tumor...these are the images I was seeing in my mind's eye lying in the hospital bed waiting for tests to begin. I am in my early thirties, how can this be happening? What went so wrong for me to be here again? Of course, I cannot help to think that it could be the very disease that took my mother from me when I was only 21 and she was 47. Internal skin cancer took her, and there I was in the hospital with abdominal issues of unknown origins. The very concerns that landed her in the same situation and under a surgeon's knife.

Here is where I had to decide. Stay this current course and find myself a client of the healthcare industry, or make a shift and discover what was making such an early display in the vision of my future lifestyle. At some point, I decided that I was not going to be dependent on external forces to control my life. It would have been so easy to continue down the traditional medicine path and let doctors and hospitals become the normal routine for the foreseeable future. As comforting as the nurses and doctors were, I soon realized that something inside of me was crying out for attention, and the way it chose to shake my reality was my health.

Being someone who was rarely ill, to now taking three prescriptions, including one that was for my heart, was a huge wake-up call for me. Granted, it was very easy to fall into a routine of taking meds throughout the day and being able to run back to the doctors or hospital for any little health 'hiccup'. I am grateful that I am very independent and realized that for all the help I received, those caregivers couldn't follow me around all my days for every possible health crisis. I had to take back the reins of my own healthcare to be fully present to all that life wanted to offer me. I thought of all the opportunities I would miss out on if I was not in control of my own being. Traveling, writing, speaking, and teaching. All these things would not be available to me globally if I couldn't leave my security blanket called modern medicine. Don't misunderstand me, I fully believe in modern medicine. I felt that for me, to teach a healthy living lifestyle, which is my passion, I must first achieve that lifestyle for myself. That is where my shift came into laser focus.

Luckily, the heart medication is one my cardiologist said I could possibly come off with certain lifestyle changes, and make those changes I did! I am happy that for over fifteen years I have been medication free. I haven't had any vaccinations or antibiotics in that time either. I don't even have a general practitioner because I am rarely ill. What a liberating feeling to not worry about filling or refilling prescriptions before a trip or adventure. What if they got lost? Could I refill them where I was going? Now all I worry about is if I will get lost on one of my adventures! That is more fun by far! Knowing that I can travel and do whatever my heart and calling brings me to because of the simple steps I put into place all those years ago is awesome-sauce! The path I chose to embark upon was not without hard work. I knew that to be different, I had to do different. That required a new thought process and again, a shift in my perception of what true health looked like.

For years, I had been under the assumption that if you looked a certain way and did specific things, that you would surely be healthy. I was wrong! I discovered a few things along my healthy journey, and this is where my passion for empowering people with tools to choose health on whatever level fits them best came forth. When I began the search for the root cause of my health issues, the first step was to a functional nutritionist who empowered and enabled me with tools and knowledge on how the body works and what I could do to take control of my health. Granted, this came easier for me to understand and implement because I had been on a path to be a medical doctor in college. I left the MD track for one in basic biology and chemistry, and I was soon to discover how important that decision would become.

So I made this decision to develop a healthy lifestyle. Now what? The decision was the easy part. It's the follow through that was difficult. Sound familiar? This is the start that stops most people. A significant shift happened for me, and I decided I was sick and tired of being sick, tired, and on medication. Any steps to improve my current situation were worth taking.

It sounds easy, right? Decide to be prescription free and in great health and voila, it's done! Not so fast grasshopper! I am not advocating coming off medication without serious consideration. There are many pills that you will have to wean off with a doctor's guidance. Fortunately for me, the ones I was taking were mostly gut related. The heart pill, however, was different. That did take some time and working with diet changes until one day I came off it and never looked back! Change is never easy. I get it. In the end, the results are so worth it!

I discovered that health is a mindset and I had been in a place where I claimed my 'diseases' and imbalances. I remember reading a passage from Dr. Wayne Dyer about not claiming your health 'issues', and I thought, *This dude is loco!* Then, I stopped and thought, *What if there is something to this?* We are conditioned to believe that we will be ill and unhealthy as we age, so it is quite natural to think that the normal progression of age equals failing health. What if I began to claim abundant health and stopped claiming illness? Could this really change my current lifestyle to one of lasting health? It was sure worth considering!

Guess what, I had a 'holy shift' moment! The moment I stopped calling gut issues 'mine' and instead said I was having minor inflammatory responses, my world changed! Now granted, I had to make some serious diet changes as well. I am not saying that you can think yourself well and still eat those burgers and fries! Suck it up buttercup – you are going to have to put in some work to achieve lasting health! (Eventually, you can enjoy the occasional burger and fries!) I was ready and willing to do whatever it took to be better than I was and have better than what I had. It was time for the real work to begin.

I am a 'get it done girl' and I always want the results right now! You can feel me on this one, right!? Decision made, results…well, they took a little longer to see. Change, while not easy, does come if you are willing to see it through. I definitely was. When I began my journey, I was at my heaviest I had ever been. As a dancer from the age of four, through college, I was always slender and didn't have much of an issue with weight gain. I would burn most anything off as soon as I consumed it during my hours of dance practice. Then life happened, as it always does. Graduation, 'real life, real job', lots of sitting and very little moving was the daily scene of my life.

Nothing good or bad happens overnight. Size 2 to size 12. I noticed it one Christmas in a family photo. All I saw were the rolls and folds in my face and torso. It was in the months following that I decided how much I wanted the change, how much I love myself, and that I was worth the struggle for better. No one appreciates all the work until the results are visible. It is true that most of us will not realize our amazing results until someone else mentions it. Then it becomes 'real'! It's the first months that are the hardest with any change. One week became one month; six months became twelve; then fifteen years later and suddenly, I am a healthy lifestyle success story!

True health and wellness are not found in monumental changes. It is in the simple steps and micro habits that I developed and implemented over time that turned into the significant lifestyle I now enjoy. Being free of disease is a choice that I make daily. I truly believe that. You may think I am foolish or full of bull. Consider this alternative; what do you have to lose by changing your beliefs to one of pure health? Being healthy on all levels has benefits beyond imagining. Moving to a state of balance and out of 'dis-ease' is well worth the steps and worth a few moments of crazy thoughts! All the change makers in the world are often thought of as crazy, so why not be crazy for yourself? Make such outstanding changes that you are now the shift for others to do the same! This is what lights my heart on fire! Being able to show people how to make small yet cumulative changes that impact their lives in unbelievable ways.

As I said before, a 10 size jump in clothing does not happen in 30 days. Nor does getting that size down. I also had to look beyond the mirror and decide what would make me the happiest. Getting to a certain pant size, or obtaining lasting health and wellness. That is a serious question and one most people fail to entertain. They want 'that size' that is revered by the media in the mirror of vanity. What I came to realize is that health does not look like a size 2, and unhealthy does not look like a size 20. More people today are ill and dying who look like what we have been conditioned to believe is the vision of health. Open any magazine, watch any TV show or movie and you will see what we are taught is health. A healthy lifestyle is so far beyond anything we can view from a screen. This is where my true shift was found, and along the way, I found my joy for life again! It didn't stem from starving myself to fit into a size 2-4. It simply came from inside of me. Realizing once again a zest for life. To achieve all that I wanted out of life I had to reinvent what a healthy lifestyle is for me. What was I willing to do for the long-term and what would best serve me in my goals toward a lifestyle of health rather than a 30, 60 or 90-day plan. I also had to change the way I looked at food. Yes, I mean really looking at food and my relationship with it. Why was I eating what I did, and more importantly, what was it doing to me in the process?

When I made that shift from mindless to mindful eating a world of changes came much easier. Simple things like eating frequently during the day, turning off the light in the kitchen after I made a plate of food, and discovering what my body/blood type needed at a cellular level ushered in a new vision of how enjoyable this new journey can really be!

As a result, I reduced the frequency and eventual need for several prescriptions, as well as numerous over the counter meds. The more grateful and appreciative I became regarding my food choices, the more effectively balanced and healthy my entire life was. I can do more and enjoy life again. I stopped wondering where I could find a place to rest at an event or even worse, always staying close to the restroom when I went out. Those with stomach issues know what I am talking about! It really puts a damper on the evening when you are not in control of your body. One of the most amazing things happened to me when I took charge of my health – I worked with instead of fighting against my body. Do you understand how freeing this is? My choices are endless. I can go anywhere, do anything and not worry if my body will give out before my will to go does. Isn't this what we all want? It's never about the size of the pants; it's about the length of time we have to wear them! I want to live life so fully that I wear holes in my clothes from going and doing!

I am reminded of the phrase, 'I can't'. It stops most people from accomplishing their life's dreams. A simple phrase that holds immeasurable weight. 'I can't lose weight'; 'I can't get rid of these allergies'; 'I can't go on that vacation because of my back, legs, etc.'. I once held onto this belief so tightly that I thought I would always be overweight and never quite well. Now I enjoy health with all the benefits of life that I can grab onto with both hands! I realized the only factor all this time that kept me from succeeding in any plan or routine, was me. I am the only thing keeping me from my vision of a healthy lifestyle. I am also the only one that can make the changes necessary to shift this vision. My decision – I am worth it! You are too. The most difficult and simplest decision is to say yes to you. How often do you say no to you and deprive yourself in the process? If you are like me, it was years of no's. No more no's! I choose to live life from a state of wellness and on my terms. I am now a happy size 6-8, traveling to speak and teach, writing books that are best sellers, and still prescription free! I am realistic about my health and wellness, and I enjoy abundant health with all the benefits of a life lived well! My journey is far from over, and I invite you to begin yours now.

Elsie Kerns

Elsie Kern's greatest passion is teaching the art of healing, which she has been doing for thirty years. Her expertise is based on extensive training with renowned healers, authors and energy pioneers, including Donna Eden and Barbara Brennan. Elsie has taught for Drexel University's complementary and integrative health program. She offers classes in Eden Energy medicine, Reiki and meditation (locally and nationally).

Elsie offers group coaching and mentors individual clients moving through personal transitions in career, relationships and health. She supports them so they can resolve long-standing issues, and live the joyful, successful life they desire.

Learn more about Elsie:

Website: www.wellnesswithelsie.com

Facebook: https://www.facebook.com/ElsieKernsWellness

Twitter: https://twitter.com/ElsieTweetsYou

Chapter 8

Housewife to Healer

By Elsie Kerns

Lost in thought, I gazed out the kitchen window, the first snow of the season was painting the perfect holiday scene, but my heart felt heavy. Christmas was Mom's favorite holiday and her chance to shine at decorating the house. My parents' passing three years ago — only six weeks apart – was a shock. However, in reality, their ill health kept signaling what was to come, even though I didn't want to see it. They had lived life to the fullest. There were no regrets, just that aching in my heart. I missed them and their physical presence. Reaching around to turn off *Good Morning America*, I was captivated by the contrast of the dolphins spinning the trainer around the water on their fins, then jumping through the hula-hoop she held up. Climbing out of the water, she extended the invitation. "You can swim with the dolphins. Call the Dolphin Research Center in Grassy Keys, Florida for details now." In 1987, swimming with dolphins was a new concept and sounded perfect for our Easter family vacation to the Florida Keys!

Sweaty palms made it a struggle to pull on my bathing suit and one whiff under my armpit confirmed that my deodorant had failed. An accelerated heartbeat and rising anxiety had me questioning this idea of swimming with the dolphins. My teenage sons were asking why Dad got to take the pictures while the dolphin swimmers were being observed by the other guests sitting in the bleachers. The trainer rounded up the ten swimmers, and everyone slipped into the water to meet the dolphins. I floated on top of the water, trying to remain calm. I could hear the sonar sounds of the dolphins beneath me as they circled gently around me. They seemed to be trying to assure me I could relax – and I did. Looking up, I saw my sons whirling around on the dolphin fins, holding the hula-hoops and swimming beside several of them. We were all lost in the magical energy. At the end of the swim, the trainer blew her whistle and called us back to the floating dock. While waiting my turn to climb the ladder, one of the dolphins suddenly popped up from the under the dock and stared at me. The trainer leaned over and whispered, "He wants you to kiss him on his bottleneck nose – go ahead!" Both reluctant and curious, I reached over and planted that first kiss on his nose. The dolphin disappeared under the water, and just as I was ready to breathe a sigh of relief, he popped back up and looked at me. Ok, a second kiss, and then a third. Finally, my turn came to climb the ladder to the dock. The pictures were a wonderful visual revisit of the swim. This past Easter, my younger son, and his wife took their sons to swim with the dolphins at the same research center.

Something magical had occurred during the swim. I had taken a risk, calmed my fears and felt more open and curious. This curiosity led me to the RAM III metaphysical bookstore in Medford. I didn't even know what the word 'metaphysical' meant or why they were using the term 'New Age'. I just knew that I had to go there. Books on Native American tradition, channeling, meditation, psychic surgeons, healing, and more beckoned. Stacked high next to my bed, I began devouring these new concepts around energy and spirituality. Having grown up Catholic, I struggled with the difference between spirituality and religion. Catholicism has a strong structure and definitive ideas while spirituality encouraged me to explore my connection to the divine within me. Learning meditation opened a quiet space internally that I never knew was there. Subtle shifts were happening, and I knew it all began with the dolphins and those kisses at the dock.

The fall Whole Life Expo being held in New York offered an option for volunteers in exchange for attending classes. The leading authors in the metaphysical field, scientists and a way-out group discussing UFOs, aliens and other paranormal phenomena headlined the event. My volunteer application was accepted, but my engineer husband was concerned about this new interest in energy. His frustration mounted as he cautioned before the expo saying, "You are falling for this crazy energy stuff. You're talking about channeling, energy vortexes and practicing meditation. And that yoga class, what is the matter with you?" Although I knew he was upset, I made the decision to go, which was unlike what I would have done in the past. My volunteer work stationed me in the breakout classrooms collecting tickets and providing the opportunity to hear each presentation. I was enthralled. On Saturday evening, a famous forgery expert, Dr. Mahoney was late getting to class, and I could see the audience growing restless, so I walked to the front of the room and announced that if Dr. Mahoney didn't show, we could talk about energy! Even I was surprised at such a bold move. Happily, Dr. Mahoney showed up at that very moment. At the end of class, one student came over and said to me, "If you want to learn about energy, the real energy chick is here this weekend, Barbara Brennan. Don't miss her workshop." Brennan was on at the end of the next day, and I had one free pass left.

Out of breath, huffing and puffing after trying to find her room, I realized I had missed the first part of her lecture, and from the back of the room, I thought her hands were glowing. Was that possible? I followed the group into the next room for her meditation. The announcer instructed us to keep our eyes closed and breathe deeply as Barbara came around to channel energy for each attendee. Harp music added to the ambiance. Positioned on the end of the row, I could feel something strong approaching me. What was it? I was afraid to open my eyes. Suddenly I felt Barbara Brennan standing next to me waving her large eagle feather over me as she said, "Fear no more woman of God." My pounding heart sensed things were never going to be the same...and they never were! Her book, *Hands of Light* detailed chakra clearing and how these energy vortexes told your life story. Her background at NASA as an astrophysicist and her scientific approach to energy clarified for me that she was the professional energy teacher to follow. Discovering she had just opened a four-year healing science training outside of New York was the final confirmation. Where do I sign up?

All hell broke loose at home. All the issues Ron and I had in the past became major issues, combined with the decision to attend the healing training slated for one week long, six times a year. How about therapy? Ron resisted fearing I would take that opportunity to annihilate him. How right he was! I couldn't wait to prove how I was right and he was wrong! We separated. My sons were upset and commented, "Mom, if you had run away with the plumber, we could explain that one...but no one gets that Barbara Brennan School of Healing!"

Out on my own at forty-six, I found myself in the same place that my parents had rented for us one summer in Medford Lakes. We lovingly referred to as the 'Hobbit'. It was the same as I remembered it. My friend's mother who lived there had passed

away suddenly, and she was not ready to sell it, so I moveu
ran off to be a healer, but I had a lot to learn about what real
healing was. I got my first lesson while working at a local nursing
home. Lyla was a hands-on administrator who was frequently out
on the floor. As she passed patients sitting in the lobby area, they
would ask the same questions repeatedly. I noticed how Lyla
stopped to answer their questions respectfully and with great
presence. Although the Brennan curriculum included various
advanced healing techniques, I began to understand that real
healing is about my ability to be present and respectful of each
individual's personal journey. I envisioned healing as this magical
instant happening. Instead, I learned it is a lifelong journey and
not about *curing* or *getting rid* of anything. The teaching that while
going through the dying process, one can be *healed* but not *cured*
made sense now. Another 'ah-ha' moment in the journey!

Another shift was about to unfold as I learned that being in body-
centered therapy was a requirement in the Brennan training.
Barbara had done personal work on herself for many years and
felt that if her students were going to work on clients, they also
needed to work on themselves. Being from an Irish Catholic
background, I had never been in therapy. The joke in my family
was that if you were going to jump off the bridge, you might
consider therapy, but only after a few beers! Core Energetics
required feeling the emotions, and expressing them in the body
for release and transformation. I began seeing things I didn't like
or want to see. Painful long buried issues in my family of origin,
my responsibility in the failed marriage and how my fears and
anxiety prevented me from being present and fully embodied
demanded my attention. These emotional experiences
overwhelmed me, raised my anxiety, questioned my self-worth
and heightened the fear around being self-supporting in the
healing profession. Confronting these issues became self-healing

– emotionally and physically. The therapy was an important part of the whole training program and contributed to exponential personal growth, which I resisted initially but valued deeply in the end and continue with today.

Running a private practice required personal and business skills I didn't have initially. I found support and mentoring through supervision sessions with a graduate of the Brennan program. Caren was a gifted healer whose creative counseling and clairvoyant insights took the healing work with clients to the next level. What I did discover as a natural gift and passion was teaching healing. I loved sharing the knowledge I had acquired from not only the Brennan training, but also Reiki, meditation, and mindfulness-based stress reduction. Continuing studies included Kabbalistic healing with the most creative teacher I've ever studied with, Jason Shulman. As Jason led us in chanting the names of God, it felt at times as though Sister Mary Agnes' authoritative voice questioned, "What are you doing now Miss McIvor?" The writings and spiritual teachings of A.H. Almaas called next for seven years in the Diamond Heart personal development program. Then, my business partner landed the just published book, *Energy Medicine* by Donna Eden in my lap.

The 2000 Kinesiology Conference was scheduled for Philadelphia. Donna was on a book tour and speaking for one day at the conference. The organizer was reluctant initially and then agreed to allow me to attend only the day of Donna's presentation. The medical profession advised Donna there wasn't anything further they could do for her MS. They suggested she get her affairs in order and arrange someone to take care of her two young daughters. Donna began her own self-healing process by applying her clairvoyant skills and working with her body's energy. She not only healed herself of MS but also created the energy medicine protocol that successfully weaved traditional Chinese medicine, kinesiology (muscle testing) and brain gym concepts together in a teachable format everyone could understand and benefit from practicing. Donna exudes a passionate and curious approach to energy work, but it is her joy that you want to reach out and grab! I loved this earthy way of teaching and working with energy. I followed her to the eight-day intensive at the Feathered Pipe Ranch in Montana, which was as magical as it sounded. Here I learned how to cross over my energies, zip-up, tap key points on my body for vitality and clear chakras easily for others and myself. This was just the beginning. Donna and her teachers had so much to offer that I was excited to learn that she opened a certification program. I organized Year One locally in New Jersey and then continued on to complete the entire four-year certification held in Arizona.

Albert Einstein stated, 'Energy is all there is'. Energy precedes the physical, so Donna developed the Daily Energy Routine to help maintain health and vitality. Life shifted when I committed to practicing the Daily Energy Routine and teaching others this five to eight-minute combination of healthy exercises. One major shift happened after realizing how much energy I was absorbing from others in a public setting, at the office, and around certain individuals. After learning and practicing the three-heart zip-up, I noticed an immediate difference in my energy level. The major 'ah-ha' my therapist helped me see was the realization that earlier in my life, I thought I could 'fix' the struggles of others around me by taking them on. I revisited the understanding that I couldn't *fix, heal* or *cure* anyone. Everyone is their own healer, and I am the facilitator. With her Daily Energy Routine, I was growing younger, not older.

The most significant shift through the practice of Eden Energy medicine was with my personal anxiety. I didn't know what to call it throughout my growing years. It occurred in social situations or speaking in class or a group. I felt shame around this struggle, which led to hyperactivity, along with rash and impetuous decisions. I developed an outer shell like the chocolate coating on popsicles, hoping no one would notice. However, when Donna Eden explained the energy perspective behind flight-fight-freeze and what could bypass this response, my world changed. Now I had easy energy options to begin changing this lifelong challenge and teach others. In today's world, the sheer pace of living, artificial electromagnetic energy and the permeating fear and violence leaves no one untouched by anxiety. When anxiety becomes a perpetual loop, it is impossible to move forward because all the body's energy is being co-opted to maintain the flight-fight-freeze response.

Humanity is transforming in the universal grid of grace and wisdom living several lifetimes and transitioning into different professional careers all in the same body. Energetically, this is efficient and possible with today's accelerated energy. However, the challenge in living longer and healthy is chronic illness. Energy medicine practices activate the body's natural healing capacity and are compatible with traditional medicine, empowering, promote wellness and are available twenty-four-seven! It is time to marry advanced medical technology and complementary/alternative energy medicine for the best health care ever.

"Energy Medicine is the oldest, safest, most accessible, most affordable energy there is."
–Donna Eden

Gina Rowe

After a turbulent childhood, drug use, and a failed marriage, Gina Rowe turned her life around and earned a degree in computer programming in her thirties. She remarried and built a new life, only to lose everything in the recession.

Determined not to give up, and driven to provide for her three boys, she's now a lead analyst in IT and an aspiring science fiction writer.

Gina considers herself a work in progress and sees all of life's challenges as learning experiences. She lives a normal life of her own making in Northern California.

Learn more about Gina:

Website: www.GinaRowe.com

Facebook: www.Facebook.com/GinaRoweAuthor/

Email: Gina@GinaRowe.com

Chapter 9

Finding Normal

By Gina Rowe

It doesn't matter how many times life tripped you up, how many times you fell down, or how many mistakes you made. Only two things matter: who are you today and who will you be tomorrow? You get to choose. If you learned from an experience, it wasn't a mistake; it was a lesson.

Most of my life I've searched for 'normal'. The truth is that whatever life you live, that becomes your normal. Isn't normal growing up with loving parents that ensure basic needs are met, boo-boos are kissed, good deeds are encouraged, and actions have consequences, all to help us grow into healthy, productive adults? That may be true in the world of Norman Rockwell, but I'll wager it's not what most experience.

People around the world live a different normal. Starvation, loved ones dying from disease and war, working in sweatshops for meager wages. Children are beaten, abused, sold into sexual slavery, and learn to fight or be killed. It sounds crazy, but that too can be normal. It shouldn't be, but if that's all you know, that creates *your* normal. Living in caves was once normal. It's how it is.

My view of normal has changed throughout life. Not all mistakes were of my own making, but enough were. Often, unresolved issues from the past lead to mistakes later in life.

I was the oldest of three. Mom and Dad were teenagers, not much older when my sister and brother were added. It was the sixties, and the vision of the normal family was changing. They divorced when I was young, and we didn't see Dad often after that; visits now and then, phone calls on holidays and birthdays. We loved him, and he loved us, but that's the way divorce went back then. It was normal.

After the divorce, we moved to a town where most people were poor. I see things now that I couldn't see then. Mom did the best she could, but she didn't have many life skills. Wedded bliss with Dad wasn't to be. She was raising three children alone. It was the seventies so 'finding yourself' and just getting by were life's priorities.

I was smart, socially awkward, overweight, and ugly. (I know, all young girls think they're ugly. I was the smart one, my sister was the pretty one. Just a fact I grew up with.) We moved over twenty times, always the new kids. My siblings made friends easily; I didn't. I did homework instead. It was something I was good at.

Due to birth order, or genetics, I was also resourceful. We lived on welfare and money was always short. I'd help figure out where to stay until we could get a new place, how to keep both lights and heat on, how to make meals from one sack of potatoes to last the rest of the month.

We lived on the wrong side of the tracks. As I got older, normal evolved into a life of drugs, alcohol, and assholes threatening each other with guns and knives at drunken parties. I was drinking and smoking pot by the age of twelve, and I was molested for years by a man who saw it was easy to take advantage of an intellectually bright and socially awkward young girl who was starved for attention. Yes, that was 'normal' too.

Although this was *my* normal, I knew it wasn't *the* normal – not what I saw on TV and in Rockwell's paintings. That was what I aspired to, but there were no road maps. I'd peek into that other world and dream of what it must be like to live there. But truthfully, deep inside I began to think I would never really belong in that world.

I believe life rests on the choices we make. Sometimes the universe splits the path in front of us, allowing a new choice, making possible what would otherwise be impossible.

By 11th grade, I was a high school dropout, making up credits at a continuation school. The unspoken goal for girls like me: try to graduate before you get pregnant. We were at a low point and Mom rented a single room in a run-down hotel, shared by the four of us. Then the universe stepped in. I was sixteen when my mom got pregnant with my youngest sister.

My stepdad took on a pregnant wife and her three teenage kids. He had a good job, didn't do drugs, didn't drink anything harder than beer, which made him laugh and never made him mean. He was a kind and gentle man.

My old perception of me clashed with my new normal life. I was smart, had developed social skills, and was now a pretty young woman, but I didn't know what to do with any of that. I took admin courses at a junior college for a year, and then moved out, got a job, paid my own bills, and joined the sexually promiscuous eighties with wild abandon.

I carried the shame from the molestation into this phase of my life. I drank too much, had too much sex with too many men. I didn't want a relationship, just sex.

One night I met a tall, handsome young man. This guy was different. We didn't have sex; he'd call me, we'd talk, go for walks, have dinner. We dated.

Now I'm older and wiser and see that attraction for what it really was. Too often, the attraction is a dangerous mix of what we want and what we believe we deserve – not what we say we deserve, but what we believe deep inside, alongside those old pictures of who we once were.

He was perfect. His dad owned a company, they went to church, ate Thanksgiving dinner from good plates, just like in Rockwell's paintings. He was attracted to my intelligence and humor… even if I wasn't pretty in his eyes. His image of me mirrored my own, and I was in love.

I look at pictures taken then, and my heart breaks for that girl. I was beautiful, but I still saw the ugly, awkward, shameful child that had been molested for years and had never told anyone.

I was determined I could be more; I could fit into his normal world, and we were happy for a while. He worked with his dad, preparing to run the business one day. He was proud when I quickly found a good job in the small town with few openings. His family loved me, and I idolized him.

His friends told him I was a good catch and he knew it, even if he didn't fully believe it. We married, but I knew in so many ways that I still wasn't quite good enough. That's when meth came into my life.

It was the perfect drug for me. I could lose weight, work full-time, clean the house, cook, help my husband's business, and still have a robust sex life with him. I was finally Superwoman!

From the outside, we looked normal. New home, two cars – it was a perfect life, except for the meth. Things got complicated when we began selling it. Not in small amounts, people coming in and out at all hours would poke holes through the Rockwell painting. We'd take large quantities to friends out of town on weekends, who then sold it to their friends.

I'd grown up with drugs and lies, but I hate lying. I'm an honest person who was good at keeping secrets. I hated my dual life. I was up day and night. I'd clean by candlelight so neighbors wouldn't know I was awake at 3 am, so things would still look normal.

Once I went five days without sleep. I went to work, played the dutiful wife, visited with family, smiled and laughed in all the right places. All while high on meth. The severe sleep deprivation made me paranoid and delusional. I was convinced police had bugged our house. I would turn off all sound and listen to light fixtures, my addled brain believing the soft hiss and garbled sounds of silence and paranoia actually formed speech patterns of people whispering on the other side of the bugging devices.

I know how crazy that sounds, but at the time, it made perfect sense to me. And the irony? We started selling drugs to make extra money. However, in a small town, the extra money would raise questions so we couldn't even spend it.

He started drinking. We'd argue; he cheated on me; he'd rage through the house, breaking things. I had never been hit by a man, and he knew I would leave if he crossed that line, but at times he would come at me, fists raised, and I would cower so he wouldn't hit me. Neither of us really wanted him to cross that line.

I don't even recognize that pathetic cowering girl today. Was it really me?

The Superwoman façade was cracking. I looked terrible. My skin was blotched, hair cracked and dry, eyes ringed with dark circles. I was thinner than I'd ever been, but I wasn't proud of it. My once-normal life was a mess, and ugly reality seeped through.

It all came crashing down in a morning raid. The police had been watching after all, but they had missed the timing – we'd dropped the last shipment and hadn't picked up the next. They confiscated scales, some cash, and a small amount of personal stash. I was handcuffed, taken to jail, booked, and released within hours.

The dual life was over. I was so relieved! With the drugs gone, I thought the drinking, cheating and verbal abuse would stop. We decided to start a family, and I became pregnant with my first son.

He continued drinking, and life got worse. His father found empty bottles in the company truck and sent him to rehab for thirty days. It turns out you can send a horse to rehab, but you can't make it stop drinking. His father fired him. He became depressed and more abusive.

One day I screamed at him, "How many times do I have to tell you I won't be married to an alcoholic!?" His calm answer stung like a slap in the face. "How many times do I have to tell you that you don't deserve anything better?"

It was true. Although he'd never said it, he had shown me in so many ways, and I had believed it. I didn't deserve the normal life I dreamed of.

I moved out of town, found a job, and my son and I shared an apartment with my brother. He continued to drink, didn't pay child support, wrecked his car, and stole mine. With both our names still on the title, the police could do nothing.

Worst of all, with the relationship over and nothing to lose, he crossed that final line. In my apartment, he choked and hit me while our four-year-old son stood helplessly watching and crying. My son, now a grown man, remembers it clearly: the panic, his inability to stop it. It left a deep scar inside him that hasn't healed. If I could change anything in my past, I would spare him that memory.

With all I've gone through, it may sound odd that's all I would change. The mistakes, humiliation, and heartbreak all came with lessons. Every experience, good and bad, has shaped who I am. At long last, I like and respect the woman I am today.

I went back to college at thirty-one, and I spent the next three years immersed in classes. I graduated with honors and received a degree in computer science. I can now care for my family without assistance.

I remarried a wonderful man who fathered our two boys and helped raise my older son. We built a life together, and lost it all in the recession in 2009 – savings emptied, foreclosure, bankruptcy, and divorce. I started over again.

After years of trying to make ends meet, I found work in IT again. I built a new life with a new love, and that relationship ended too. I was once told that every relationship will emd, or it will be the person you spend your life with. Those really are the only two options, but I remain friends with those I loved because they brought value to my life, and that doesn't change by living apart.

Given time, it has all come together. Dad and I rebuilt our relationship, and now I cherish the time I spend with him and my stepmom. I see Mom and my stepdad often; they are a big part of my life. After my sister, they had a son. I enjoy close relationships with all four of my siblings.

With the help of a group of women, I slowly eroded those deep-held, negative ideas of what I deserved and who I was. As with all hard tasks in life, I couldn't have accomplished that alone.

Now mid-way through my fifties, I've recreated normal with new priorities: family, especially time with my boys; I make memories instead of acquiring things; bills are paid, savings are growing. I live frugally and invest in vacations with my boys while they're still willing to spend time with Mom. If it's not broke, don't replace it, and if it's worth keeping, fix it. The same goes for relationships.

Good or bad, things always change. As I write this, I'm recovering from depression. Nothing bad happened – I woke up one morning to devastating sadness, and it stayed for almost two months. I had to admit there was something wrong, take time off work, and learn yet again that I am not Superwoman. If you don't learn the first time around, the universe will keep presenting challenges, refreshing your memory, providing another chance to get the lesson.

And that attention-starved girl who was molested? I believed all my life that I understood 'my part' in it. I had needed the attention; I couldn't bear the look I'd see in the eyes of others if I told, especially in my mother's eyes; and it would have changed our then-normal life. I didn't want to carry that burden. Instead, I carried guilt and shame, allowing them to shape my own worth for almost forty years.

Sometimes a single phrase is all it takes. I saw a therapist a few years ago, and he asked a question that changed my life, brought peace to the years of torment. "Could you have moved out and lived on your own?"

The question took me by surprise. "Well, no," I stammered.

"Then you had no part in it. You were a child. Someone did something they shouldn't have done – to a child. You played no role in it."

I thought long and hard about that. In my mind, even as a child, I had been an adult. Once I was grown, I viewed my past through the lens of an adult, but I *had* been a child. This freed me from the guilt and shame I'd held onto throughout my life, for something that was not mine to hold.

Perspective is the key to everything; it will shape your vision of normal.

Haritha Yalavarthi

Haritha Yalavarthi is a desk jockey and a mother to two boys. She is passionate about mentoring and coaching young women while balancing demands of work and family. Haritha is a creative who loves to find ways to soothe her soul by pursuing her passion for running, hiking, reading, and baking. She has lived in India, the US and Taiwan, and is a student of life, cultures and human psychology.

Chapter 10

Tight Rope Walker

By Haritha Yalavarthi

I followed the unfamiliar voice. "Your daughter will have a troubled marriage," I heard as I walked in on my parents' conversation with the family astrologer. My curiosity (as any ten-year old's would) quickly turned from wanting to hear more of the conversation to the kids playing outside. I ran outside leaving my parents and the astrologer drone on about my seemingly distant wedded life and the possibility of future events. Maybe that seed of doubt had a bigger impact than I had given it thought or credit. Perhaps it shaped the way I chose to find love and even felt a twinge of hope that I could control my destiny of 'troubled marriage' when my family moved to the states.

Moving from India to the US at the age of seventeen suddenly presented a world of opportunity to not only be able to pursue higher education but also find a job and be financially independent. After I had moved, I got a part time job, got into a good school, graduated with an engineering degree, and landed a good job. I had a good head on my shoulders and dated (under my parents' disapproving eye) in the hope of finding love. I wanted to find a partner and change my supposed destiny to troubled marriage. I fell in love, but after moving to a new city for work, the relationship didn't withstand the difficulties of a long distance relationship. I threw myself into work, working out, running, rock climbing, and finding new friendships.

Shortly into this journey of my new life as an educated, independent, self-sufficient young adult recovering from heartbreak, I met a man that was everything I had hoped for. We fell in love, hard and fast, and planned a lifetime together. With an air of arrogance, I shook the dirt off my shoulder that I was about to overscore the script of troubled marriage predicted by an astrologer some fifteen years earlier. In the simmering desire to prove to myself, I ignored the cracks in our relationship.

Together we were building a family of our own. Strongly believing in giving enough breathing room for each other to grow, we charged forward. I was excited to have someone that would encourage me to pursue my own dreams and support me along the way. We made compromises for each other along the way. I continued to strengthen my 'never give up' trait. When hard times hit, I tried harder, ignoring my gut instincts and trying with all my might to deal with whatever life threw at me.

Surprisingly we made it through all the up and downs – the financial, emotional, and physical burdens of renovating a home with a new baby in tow. In our classic fashion of tackling bigger goals each time, we wanted to be a one working parent household. So we planned, and with some reluctance, I agreed to try living in India. We had enough money saved to live there cheaply for a few years, raise our young family and maybe even start a business of our own.

My husband quit his job, we sold the house we lovingly put together and moved our things into storage. I took a three-month sabbatical from work while I was eight weeks pregnant with our second child, and off we went to India. If the first three months went well, I was to quit my job to live there semi-permanently. The only way we were going to give up on this plan was if any one of us had health issues that would put our lives at risk.

Well, our twenty-month old was the first to catch a stomach bug of some sort, the poor little guy kept getting worse each day. We could've gone to a bigger city for emergency treatments, but we wanted a peaceful life in the smaller cities. So we held on, keeping a close watch on the little fellow. He was in good spirits and active but wasn't keeping any food down. We learned a lot in the nineteen days of being in India tending to our child (who still was unable to keep anything down) and staying indoors to give his immune system time to adapt and fight his stomach issues.

I felt unusually nauseous that night, being ten weeks pregnant, I wrote it off as an exceptionally bad case of morning sickness. Woken up by serious cramping I realized that I had picked up whatever my son had been dealing with. The next morning we collectively and unemotionally decided that we would return to the US, scrapping our months of planning and a dream for a simpler life. It wasn't such a bad thing – we consoled ourselves, I still had a job I could return to. It would be difficult, but it wasn't anything we couldn't handle. However, I didn't realize that the shattered dream had left one of us more emotionally wounded than the other.

We came back to the US with a few more weeks to spare before I had to return to work, so we took a road trip to see the vast landscapes of the western United States. Fighting morning sickness and reality of returning to work as now the sole breadwinner for the family, I ignored everything else. I focused on moving forward. I pushed hard, sometimes I cried but thought it was the pregnancy hormones making me more emotional. We welcomed our second child, and I returned to work after my six-week maternity leave. I didn't allow myself time to be disappointed. I went through the motions of life but didn't enjoy much of it, as being the family breadwinner, and a working mom, wasn't something I had ever planned to do. Taking a page from the book *The little engine that could* that I read to the boys every night, I repeated to myself, *I think I can, I think I can.* Inherently ignoring the fabric of discord that was quietly weaving itself. As I dug myself out of my post-pregnancy haze, I found myself in a life raft, slowly drifting away to an island devout of emotional flora and fauna.

I didn't allow myself the freedom to feel whatever sorrow, anger or discomfort that was within me. I woke up each morning and did what I needed to do to set out for the day. I disregarded my own voice calling out for help, and ignored my husbands' struggle as he put his life back together. However, occasionally those embers of discord flared into a raging fire, and the small cracks in the relationship started to gain strength. When I tried to voice my concerns, I sounded like a lunatic that wanted to be Superwoman saving the world, and a wife that wanted to be a mother tending to her kids.

I often found myself at a crossroads of trying to decide which camp I landed on. Instead of deciding, I vowed to be both a career woman and a supermom. We were presented with an opportunity to go overseas to work for a few months, and I managed to take the family with me. While there, we enjoyed it and were given a chance to live there for a few years. Figuring that this would allow us to give our young family an opportunity to live in a different culture like the one we planned in India. We jumped at the chance. It was the happy medium, Taiwan was far less risky than India, and I was moving there with a job, so we felt more at ease. However, I was still uneasy that we were putting my husbands' career on the slow burner, but he reduced my anxiety with plans to continue his new budding career plan as a photographer. Leaving the unease to the winds we moved, managed it all quite nicely and mindfully masking the growing cracks between my husband and me.

I shushed the doubting voices in my head, turning to my favorite thing in the world – early morning running and being active while focusing on the things that were going well. *People would kill to be in your shoes*, I told myself on every one of those early morning runs. Feeling that this lackluster marriage wasn't unique to me but familiar to most families with young children, I walked the tightrope that family life had become. I started to emotionally close up and drift off.

Do you ever get that feeling that when you are intentionally stalling, the universe just has a way of slapping you in the face and make you jump? I thought I had learned and grown a lot, but the universe was hell bent on teaching me things I was refusing to learn.

My kids and husband spent the summer in the US while I stayed in Taiwan working, catching up with friends and activities, including an annual health checkup. "There is mass in your breast that you should have looked at," said the ultrasound tech, to which I quickly noted that it had been bothering me and that I would have mammogram soon.

With a zooming career, being relatively young, and having no family history, I was shocked to be diagnosed with breast cancer. This news was not a bump I was prepared for, and it wasn't in my control. Despite my healthy lifestyle, my body had failed me. It wasn't a case of in-the-moment-anxiety making the molehill look like a mountain; it was indeed a mountain that appeared out of thin air.

Unlike all the previous bumps we endured together standing on an emotionally strong foundation, I knew I was about to endure this one in a life raft closer the emotionally deserted island devout of flora and fauna. However, I didn't have the luxury of time or capacity to build that foundation again. I had to make decisions where to have the surgery, which tests to have done and whether to have a double or a single mastectomy. I focused on getting past the surgery, recovering, and nothing else. That was the only way I could wake up each morning. I had to be there for the kids, I had to be strong for them. So I did what I had to do to get past the immediate tasks at hand only focused on what I could control. The aftermath of the surgery was when the real spiral downward started. The physical recovery was the easy part, but the emotional recovery had turned for the worse.

With each little bump we got past, I realized that my husband and I both lost a little of ourselves. I held onto the belief that should the day come that I no longer could support the family I wanted someone to rely on...someone that could step up. He held onto the belief that he was supporting my dream to break that career glass ceiling. Then, post-surgery, with the emotional stability comparable to a fleeting dandelion seed, I walked away from everything. I wasn't willing to put my own needs on the back burner; it wasn't my responsibility to nurse someone out of depression. I wanted to rely on him, but he was not as I remembered or *wanted* to remember. We hung on together for a few more months to watch depressingly as the marriage fall apart. We argued, dined together, yelled, cried, reasoned with each other, and went to therapy together. One deafening silent treatment after another led to us falling apart. It was if I was watching my life come apart in slow motion.

I write my story in hopes to make sense and reason with pain. If even one person could benefit from my learnings I could find sense in it all. I wish to lend my shoulders to someone that could learn from my mistakes.

The two years of greatest sorrow also have been the greatest source of growth. Summing up a few years' worth of growing into a short list isn't possible, but there is beauty in simplifying it all. Here is what has served me well so far.

Honor your gut instinct: give your gut the respect it deserves. Understand the difference between fear and gut instinct. Ask yourself, what is my gut telling me? Write it out truthfully, even if it is painful. Ask yourself if it's the truth before you let that thought swirl in your head and cause a never-ending loop of doubt.

Sleep and learn to breathe. Get some rest! Sleep doesn't suddenly make your problems go away, but it does help you handle problems with a clear head. I learned this the hard way. I woke up every morning at 4 am only having had four hours of sleep. It caught up with me, and I found myself in a constant state of stress - unable to deal with minor issues with perspective. Count to six while breathing in and eight while breathing out. This helps signal your brain to not be in fight or flight mode.

Physical activity. Find a way to exercise, every day. Despite being an active person, in times of conflict, I found myself too drained to run or even gather myself for a walk. I didn't realize the power of a run until I called my sister one day crying, only to call her back a few days later feeling gleeful. I had realized that running in the morning put me in a better state of mind. Get moving!

Ask for help. Let others help you. I used to say to people that if you found out that a friend was suffering, wouldn't you want to help them? If so, then why is it so hard for us to ask for help?

Asking for help allowed me to acknowledge the troubles and get out of my own head.

Build you. Unapologetically build yourself first. You are of no ✿ service to anyone if you are not together yourself. It's ok to cry but don't cry all day, it is normal to want to retreat but don't set up home there.

In my short amount of time on this planet, I have experienced the roller coaster of life. Despite my strength, the universe continues to break me. I am humbled by each break and vow to stand strong accepting that I will break again. Pass on your intelligence, there is a purpose for your suffering. I lean upon others that have struggled before me and will lend a shoulder to those that will struggle after me. One can only bow to the circle of life.

Joan Hughes

Joan Hughes is a highly sought international expert on the elimination of money-blocks. She gained her reputation by helping entrepreneurs easily remove their invisible income ceiling.

Having had a charmed life and successful business career serving the private and public sectors, Joan suddenly lost everything she had built. After ten slow, painful years, she finally discovered the cause of her devastating losses when she uncovered and eliminated the hidden blocks to money and success that she unknowingly harbored for decades.

Today, Joan helps coaches, consultants, and entrepreneurs free themselves of the hidden barriers to their own advancement and prosperity.

Learn more about Joan:

Email: joan@InnerPathSolutions.com

Recording of story: http://InnerPathSolutions.com/trials-triggers-transcendence/

Facebook: https://www.facebook.com/innerpathsolutions/

Chapter 11

Trials, Triggers, and Transcendence

By Joan Hughes

On September 1st, 2006, my husband and I drove away from Harmony Lane, the dream home that we had designed and built, where we had lived for eleven happy years, and we headed for the city in silence, knowing it was the last time we would ever see our beloved house.

It may seem strange to call a house 'beloved', but it was our creation, born out of our minds, emotions, bodies, and especially our hearts.

We had come to the idea together, not long after we met, to fulfill our shared dream to leave the city and live in nature. During trips to France and Mexico, we had lovingly gathered visual inspirations for the home we would build. Out of these travels and years of imaginings, our home had been born, a straw-bale house on the top of a hillside, with expansive views through birches and pines onto Long Lake, bringing nature into our home and us into nature.

It's octagonal-shaped living spaces and perfect proportions instilled peace and harmony into every inch of the home, and we enjoyed visits in all seasons from foxes and deer, who made our property their home, and spent many quiet evenings listening to the loons call as we watched the moon rise over the lake.

So why had our dream come to this end?

A friend once said to me, "Whatever you touch turns to gold." I can see how that might have appeared true to him. I'd had an eclectic career. I *had* been lucky when it came to money. For many years, whatever I asked for did appear in my life, almost as if I had a magic genie.

I was never a big spender, but there was always enough for me to follow my greatest joy, traveling. I had lived a year in France, spent four summers sketching the beauty of the Greek Islands, wintered in Mexico and California, and visited many other countries in Europe and the Middle East.

My career had been fun and creative. Since I wanted to be free, above all else, I decided to work for myself. I worked with a variety of organizations – instructing students at the university, giving writing workshops to auditors and foreign service officers in government, and executives in the pharmaceutical industry. I even worked with an ambassador needing help with his English. Being self-employed allowed me to have summers off and be available to my son on his holidays while he was growing up.

I had dreamed of being an artist, and in the eighties, I left my twenty-five-year career in communications and became a professional artist for nine years. I had also fortuitously created a generous nest egg through owning and selling the homes that I'd lived in. Every move I made had been a step above the last one.

I put freedom before ambition, and I did pretty well.

Still, I was full of contradictions. Despite my seeming success, I carried within myself crushing feelings of self-doubt and ever-present fear that something bad was about to happen, which caused me to play smaller than I was capable of, never allowing myself to go full out with my inborn talents in the work I was doing.

There are people who are born with a clear knowingness of what they have come into life to do. Their confidence and clarity are often evident when they are young. They may be found sitting at a piano composing music at the age of three and never stray from this path, or they may see themselves as leaders and take direct steps toward fulfilling that vision in their lifetime.

That is not my story.

Mine is one of feeling lucky that I made it to where I am today. It's a circuitous route that landed me in unforeseen pits and traps. But from this end of the journey, I can understand exactly why it all unfolded as it did, and I am grateful that, despite the challenges I may have created for myself, I have been kept healthy and safe and magically protected through it all.

So why the surprising turn in my fortunes?

It's extremely difficult for me to write about this. For years, I have blamed myself for what happened, and writing about it can still fill me with shame and regret, even though I now know better.

After our first years at the lake, we began to get into debt. Our property taxes had risen precipitously, and I had also started a business that was costing more than I was making. Being a stranger to debt and having always been 'lucky with money', I had never learned how to manage my finances. So I followed the advice of a friend and took out a small mortgage on our home, using the equity to pay off the debt. Not long after, we were back in debt again. I increased the mortgage a second time. By the third increase in the mortgage (trying to turn my business around), I finally heard what my husband had been saying for two years. We *had* to sell our house to stop the bleeding.

If that wasn't enough, once we were in the city, our challenges continued. I became really concerned about our dwindling savings. Like an injured creature flailing around in the water, I was found by several sharks smelling blood, and during the next few years, I 'gave away' what was left of our nest egg to sophisticated investment scammers, two of whom came with good reputations.

There we were, in our sixties, starting all over again, and I had caused it all to happen.

To make up for it, I spent the next ten years working hard to help to recover the savings that had been lost. I was going to 'save the day'. I earned advanced certification in an energy healing modality and had a full practice. Then I switched to business coaching, where I transferred the techniques and expertise I had gained to helping clients double and triple their profits in business.

But I, myself, still wasn't able to get ahead.

I was a successful coach, but that had come with substantial financial outlays on products and programs to help me rebuild a 'nest egg' for our old age. No matter what I did, it wasn't enough. Once again, I was creating debt.

It was ten years since we had been forced to give up our dream home. I was stuck, and there were many nights when I would be haunted by pictures of being old and poor.

I was a bad money-manager. I had made and continued to make poor financial decisions. It was mystifying. Why was this happening, when the first six decades of my life had been so lucky?

Was there something causing *me* to create my money problems?

One day, I remember shaking my fist at the universe and saying, "Enough of this! I want things to be back to the way they used to be!"

Then in March of 2016, I heard about a concept that I hadn't been aware of before – 'money-blocks'. These were energies, memories, beliefs, images, and emotions that have been 'trapped' in our subconscious minds and, if we have enough of them, they can be triggered and start to interfere with our lives. Further, they can be cleared so that they never interfere again. What a revelation.

I was already doing energy work in my coaching practice. All I had to do was to apply it to my financial situation, and perhaps I would be able to free myself of what was lurking in my subconscious and causing me to squander the nest egg I had been so blessed with.

I immediately set out to become accomplished at using an amazing technique that would allow me to uncover and eliminate my own 'hidden money-blocks' and the underlying causes at the base of my recent financial losses.

Using this modality, I uncovered past influences that had been hiding within me all of my life. It was these subconscious influences that had started blocking money in my life. I was harboring over thirty 'hidden money-blocks'.

During March, April, and May of 2016, I eliminated all of my hidden blocks to money and success. Remarkably, I felt happier, lighter, more confident, and it even showed up in our bank account. My income doubled within a few months. I had finally broken through my lifelong invisible income ceiling.

After they were all cleared, I suddenly had a mind-blowing epiphany. I needed to stop blaming myself completely for what had happened. It was not all my fault. I could see that the losses I experienced in my life had been inevitable. It had only been a matter of time.

You see, I had lived with these hidden 'time bombs' in my subconscious mind since I was a baby. This may seem strange, but even when we are very young, we are being influenced by the people around us and can carry these bombs throughout our lives.

For the most part, it was the fears and the beliefs around money of my dear grandfather that came up. Despite having gone through The Depression and having managed to set himself up as a successful tailor after WWII, he suffered from grave self-doubt, and I unknowingly absorbed his despair like a sponge.

So his beliefs, his doubts, and fears became mental and emotional landmines just waiting to be triggered within me. Finally, I could see why they had been triggered at that time in my life when I had previously been so lucky.

My own fears. My own doubts.

When we moved into our home at the lake, I began to harbor a secret fear, the fear that we wouldn't have enough money as we grew older. That wasn't a new fear to me. When I was an artist in my forties, I remember having thoughts about being a bag lady. They were irrational. I was doing extremely well at the time. That fear grew within me and, over time, it led me to make financial decisions and choices that moved us toward the very thing I was trying to avoid – one financial loss after another until we had lost everything we had created.

Many people have wondered how I was able to go on, and I will soon share the most important shift I experienced throughout our period of losses. For now, I can say that the greatest gift of doing this energy work was my acceptance that it wasn't entirely my fault. Thanks to clearing my money-blocks, I was able to understand that I had been inadvertently programmed from childhood. I hadn't chosen that, but I could now choose to follow a different path.

I'm going to end my story here, with a powerful experience I had on the day when I finally admitted and accepted that my husband and I had to let go of our dream home. I had been fighting against that day coming for two years, each year putting us deeper and deeper into debt, while I tried everything I could think of to turn things around.

As I remember this experience, I am right back there, sitting on the edge of our bed looking through the French doors onto the patio and through the trees to the blue, sparkling water of the lake. I am saying to myself, *I will not let this take me down.*

I realize that I have to let go of all I hold dear. We will have to sell the house so that we can pay off our debts. We will move back to the city and find a place to rent.

I sense that falling into hopelessness over this deep disappointment is a real possibility, but out of some part of my being comes the thought that this is just a material possession. There are other things in my life that are much more precious to me. If I lost *them*, this house and dream would fade into a very small place in my life.

So I force myself to imagine losing what is *truly* precious to me, the people I love, who love me.

One by one, in my imagination I let them disappear from my life.

"What if I lost my son? What if I lost my mother? What if I lost my husband? My grandchildren. My brothers..." I go through each one slowly, until I've got to the end.

No loved ones left. No friends left. Nobody I know and care about. I am alone. Nothing left. The home was gone. Possessions were gone. Just emptiness. Silence.

Then it hits me. *I* am here. I'm *alive*. I am a *creator*. I've done this before; I can do it again.

This is where I am today.

I am cleared of what has been blocking me my whole life. The path before me is clear. My inner being is open and free to attract and create all the good I desire in my life. Most importantly, my heart is filled with gratitude for everything that has happened, and for everything that is about to unfold.

I can see now that it was all bound to happen at some time in my life. At some point, the fear that was lurking inside me was going to trigger those little hidden 'land mines', and I was going to end the luck that I had been blessed with. It was inevitable, given the hidden money-blocks I was living with.

Do I wish it had never happened? Yes, but that was not in my hands, and so I am thankful that it happened when I was in my sixties and not when I reached my eighties. Thank goodness I still had time to recreate myself and my life.

My biggest takeaway from all that I have gone through? The resilience that we all have built into us.

"It's not easy being green," as a famous frog once sang. Well, it's not easy being human either, but thankfully, we are all creators. We are powerful. We are resilient. This gives us our brilliance – our ability to go through adversity and come out the other side, better than before. Each challenge we face, each crisis we overcome, brings us to a higher and higher level of awareness, consciousness, and joy.

Sometimes, the bigger the challenge, the harder the fall and the harder the fall, the bigger the recovery. There are times now when I experience such deep gratitude for life that the bliss I am filled with can bring tears to my eyes. It can come at most unexpected times – while I'm showering and feeling blessed by the water that flows freely over me. Or even while washing dishes and marveling at the abundance of dish soap, chairs to sit on, cupboards to store things in… I could go on.

I ask myself. Do we have to learn from adversity? It appears so, but maybe not forever. As one who has grown immensely from adversity, I now put my intention out to the universe:

"Ok. Thank you. You've got through to me. I get it. Now, I am ready to learn through joy."

Joshua Bloom

The trusted authority on the application of quantum healing, and the host of Emotionally Free TV, Joshua Bloom is featured on the front-page of The Washington Post as one of the first coaches ever to be featured in the mainstream media.

Joshua has developed his own healing modality called Quantum Energy Transformation™, a way of being called Being Quantum™, a healing process called Age Clearing™, his own reiki modality named Being Reiki™, and an allergy elimination process called Quantum Allergy Release™.

He is an author, speaker, movie producer, master facilitator, trainer, and for many, a go to emotional freedom master.

Learn more about Joshua:

Website: www.EmotionallyFree.TV

Facebook: www.Facebook.com/groups/EmotionallyFreeTV

Free Gift: www.TheUltimateAnswerMovie.TV

Chapter 12

The Quantum Shift

By Joshua Bloom

In my early thirties, I realized that something was different. Something had changed. I wasn't sure what, but I knew that I didn't feel safe in my world anymore. I kept getting signs and signals letting me know something was wrong. That fear became stronger, upping the ante until I had no other choice but to pay attention to it. The energy was welling up inside me; it was too late. I was experiencing anxiety attacks so large they would take me over, and I would feel helpless. I had no idea how I could fix this. I felt I was in *way* too deep.

With a background in coaching, healing, and energy work, I had recently been recognized in a front-page Washington Post article as one of the first coaches featured in the mainstream media. I thought I had made my mark, and I was awaiting the wondrous fairytale success of an entrepreneur, but I didn't know what I was in for. *This is where my journey truly began.*

My life was becoming smaller and smaller. Being alone was so frightening that I hired someone to be with me at times just to make sure I wouldn't freak out with fear. I was afraid to be alone, and even more scared to move forward in my life. I was even afraid to walk around the block. I thought I was going crazy! However, I wasn't about to give up!

I took class after class, program after program, and learned every healing modality possible to help me eliminate this immense fear: *nothing worked*. I worked with many healers, spiritual teachers and energy workers trying to get my life back – all to no avail. Some days were bearable while others were worse. I did my best to move forward even though the thought of turning this mess around seemed so impossible.

I visited a hypnosis center searching for relief, only to realize they could not help me feel safe in my world. However, I realized that I could help them with my knowledge of neuro-linguistic programming, healing, and energy work. So I began to work at the center, thinking it would take my attention off myself and onto helping others. I hoped this would help me find a resolution for my *immense* fear.

One of my very first clients came to me, saying she had fibromyalgia. I had no idea what she was talking about. It was like she was speaking a different language: fibro-my-al-what? She told me that this syndrome was incurable, but her intuition had guided her to me. I was skeptical, but I said I would help her. I asked her a simple question that she had never been asked before. It took her by surprise, and she started to cry. I held her hands and connected with her at a deep level. I asked her to breathe, and she engaged the energy in her body for about four minutes. "It's gone!" she said, out of the blue. "What's gone?" I asked. "The fibromyalgia left my body!" she said. I didn't know who the crazy one was at this point, as nothing so dramatic and profound had ever happened to me before. While feeling shaky and unsure, but with pseudo-confidence, I said, "Oh great!" I was filled with excitement for her transformation and hoping she would not notice that I was taken aback, unsure of what had just happened.

The next day she called me and explained how great she felt and how grounded in her body she was. She said she hadn't felt this way in over sixteen years. Can you imagine? She had fibromyalgia symptoms for over sixteen years, and in just four minutes, her world had changed so dramatically. I realized this was not a dream. Her fibromyalgia symptoms were truly gone. She was free from the confines of this debilitating and incurable syndrome. While her experience was truly amazing, and I helped her well beyond what anyone would think is possible, there was no greater transformation than what she gave me. I gained a sense of hope and drive that I had never felt before. It provided me with the energy to continue moving toward helping others at this extraordinary level, and opened the possibility to fully heal myself. Transformation is possible!

I felt like I had a special secret about the world that no one knew about. It was as if I had stepped out of the 'Matrix'. With a strong sense of accomplishment, I knew something great was about to happen; I didn't know what or when, but I knew. *This was the moment where I realized that anything was possible!* My life was forever changed! My life from this point would never be the same. I had evolved.

My plan worked better than I had ever imagined. Using intuition as my guide, I mixed and matched neuro-linguistic programming with energy work, and saw amazingly profound results. Clients with anxiety, migraines, fibromyalgia and more, became free from their symptoms quickly and many times – instantly. Hypnotists at the center wondered what I was doing to get such amazing and profound results. From this, my modality, QET™ was born.

Although my clients quickly became free, I still went home with my anxiety, living in my unsafe world, and wondering why nothing was working for me. I was stuck emotionally and had many physical problems, none of which resolved.

I engaged healing for myself in many ways, failing most of the time. I didn't 'get it'! As other people healed quickly, I just felt more stuck. Then I realized I could see in others what they could not see in themselves. I could find the root cause of their issue and help them transform it.

When it came to my own healing and transformation, well, that was another story! I could not see my own issues. My patterns and habits were invisible to me. I had to find another way of seeing myself. In a lightbulb moment, I received a message to act as my own practitioner – and to *play!* I completed a session as if I were my own client and began to see the same amazing results. The truth was, I *could* now heal myself! I realized that I was the one limiting my life experiences. I felt like Dorothy from *The Wizard of Oz*. The answers were *always* with me, yet I required the journey in order to see them.

I continued teaching, helping others, and shifting the fear for myself. I kept stepping out of my comfort zone, each time realizing that I was safe in my own world. Now, like my clients and students, new possibilities were available to me too! My world opened as I learned to transform energies, ultimately changing my 'beingness' and my life! I became a new person. What *magic*! What amazingness!

Then I discovered a healing modality has 'the model' embedded within it. It was invisible to me until I looked closer. The medical and therapy models for healing imply that we are in victim mode and are setup in a way that says we need to be fixed. This made me feel that something within me was broken and needed to be fixed. Just as I did, we all automatically adopt these common models without question, as we are born into them.

The holistic community also offers many modalities. I thought they were holistic in nature, but hidden under the guise of this structure is the therapy model as the backbone, reinforcing the idea that I'm broken and need to be fixed.

Reiki was all about drawing and memorizing symbols. It focused on the details. What you do, and how do you do it. It took me to my head, and although this was energy work, the energy part took a back seat. Quite disappointing.

I tried hypnosis, learning that I could be in a trance, yet still be in my head, and out of my body. This was not healing at all. Yes, I could make changes on a more superficial level, but since I was disconnected, I was not able to get to the root of the issue. I also needed the practitioner in order to solve the problem. I felt dependent on someone else to help me, which made me feel more powerless.

I even tried EFT (the Emotional Freedom Technique). I tapped every day for months, only to find that EFT only works with one aspect of the problem at a time. When I realized I had thousands of aspects to deal with, I quickly felt stuck, became overwhelmed, and really discouraged. These strategy-based techniques and protocols were not what I was looking for. I needed something to work. Something *easy*, that had the ability to get to the deeper levels and the root causes of my issues.

Best-selling author and scientist, Bruce Lipton, Ph.D. taught me that I was either in growth or protection. Being in protection is being caught up in your own fear and living defensively, always trying to protect yourself from any danger. It's impossible to move forward or grow from this therapy model perspective.

Being in *growth,* on the other hand, meant I could be open, curious and playful.

Here's what I did to try and help myself: I brought up an issue to work on, but most of the time the issue was right in front of my face. I tried to relax my body in hope that I could calm down and invite healing. I breathed and opened space in my body. I waited for energy movement and healing. I breathed more, and sometimes for over two hours.

I did all of this... and nothing. I was *devastated!* I tried and failed. Then I realized I was working from a therapy/fix it model perspective. I wanted to give up, but I kept trying, and you can too!

I chose the model that would get me a positive outcome. I needed to be in growth rather than protection in order to heal and transform my debilitating issues. These understandings made it possible to move forward and have excellent focus. I felt more confident and excited to tackle my biggest issues, knowing I was on the right track. Yet, fear still lingered and failure prevailed until I got back on track.

Then it happened, an insight came over me, telling me I had no ground, no connection to myself. I realized when I worked with other people, I could use their ground, and it helped calm me down. However, if I was alone, I would feel unsafe and scared. In the end, I learned healing was possible for me. For it to truly work, I would need to develop a ground: a connection to myself that I had been missing for years, but never knew it.

The next time I set out to heal myself. It *worked!* I was able to release a serious panic attack, in the moment. For the first time, I saw results beyond my expectations. Yes! Healing was possible!

I continued healing other emotional and physical issues until I shifted my migraine headaches, attention deficit disorder, major fear and anxiety, and other major problems. I remember the precise moment when I got my life back! I want you to get your life back too.

Quantum Energy Transformation™ helped me to release and transform information stored in my body at the cellular level. This energy shifted into a more useful life experience so I could live a life of joy and happiness. It all happened through eight important 'knowings'.

1. Moving my *attention* from my analytical mind to my tailbone is key to accessing the cellular structure of my body for a permanent quantum change. Where I put my attention matters when it comes to quantum change. Attention is extremely important and necessary to elicit movement and flow in my body at the root of my personal reality.

2. From my personal experiences of deep healing, I know the amazing power of *connection*, which I can access within myself, by staying deeply grounded in my body to invite openness, movement and flow. I begin this process simply by moving my attention from the thinking mind, down to the base of my spine (the tailbone).

3. *Intention* is an aspect of my intuition that requires that I be in the energy of my higher self, not stuck in my thoughts. As I continue to use my attention, I invite a deep connection to my higher self and ground deeply into my body. I then move into a new perspective of the quantum field, filled with many more possibilities for my unfolding self.

4. *Allowing* is how I 'let go' or 'accept what is' in my life. Many times, I would get in my own way, sabotaging what I choose

to have in my life. Allowing opens space in my body creates the relaxation response and instantly puts me at ease. Now my intention shifts from an idea and becomes a part of my new reality.

5. Just as the moon and the wind are forces that cause waves in the ocean, *breathing* and intention move the waves of energy through my body. This creates a cellular change within me at the deep structure of my cells, allowing new possibilities to transcend into my new reality.

6. From the moment of connection, my body begins to open and create space, while my intention and breathing promote movement through this *openness*. These mechanisms allow for a permanent quantum shift in the deep structure of my cells.

7. *Movement and flow* allow for openness in my body and becomes possible when I am in my body, leading me into the quantum shift.

8. I discovered that we don't need to believe any of this for QET™ to work. Simply being open to the *possibility* allows us to attract the outcomes we are seeking.

Transformation happens for me when stagnant energy in my body moves freely. As it moves, it shifts and changes, raising my frequency and becoming love energy that supports my growth and movement forward. Instead of being triggered, I feel stable, solid and supported by this new energy that has become like a rebirth.

When I experience a release, it's much like transformation: energy leaves my body and is no longer present. My system uses the innate intelligence of my body to recalibrate my energy system, with a shift that brings in new energy at the highest frequencies of 'beingness', allowing me to feel supported, alive and balanced.

Quantum Energy Transformation™ is simple, easy and effective. I used QET™ to shift the fear and uncertainty in my unsafe world into a new spiritual connection for myself, and now I feel wonderful! I want the same for you!

Breathing + Attention + Connection + Intention + Allowing + Openness + Movement and Flow + Possibility = *The Quantum Shift*.

Judith Richey

Judith Richey brings holistic healing to the mainstream and helping people find peace, balance and wellness. The creator behind 'Your Well-Being Guide', a practice incorporating energy work, aromatherapy and well-being coaching, Judith guides clients to live a life free of blockages and disease.

After leaving what looked to the world like a rewarding career in financial services, Judith learned the secrets to living life on her terms, with complete serenity and bliss. She now guides others to break through their barriers and find their life path.

Utilizing her academic training and degrees along with numerous holistic certifications, Judith infuses her dedication to healing with passion and intuitive expertise. Her journey is your journey, and she is there to guide you every step of the way.

Learn more about Judith:

Website: www.judithrichey.com

Facebook: https://www.facebook.com/yourwellbeingguide

Instagram: https://www.instagram.com/yourwellbeingguide

Chapter 13

What Dreams May Come

By Judith Richey

When I was a young woman in my early twenties, I had the most fascinating dream. I was taken to see God, in the back of a large army truck – the kind of truck soldiers ride in. We rolled up to a large building, with a sweeping staircase and huge double doors. Jesus met us at the bottom of the stairs and came to the back of the truck to help us unload and come into the building. I was taken to a library and marveled at the expansiveness and number of volumes there. God came in to see me. To me, He looked like the TV actor, Lorne Greene, from a show I watched as a little girl called *Bonanza*. God (a.k.a. Lorne Greene) took me all around the library and told me to study. To learn everything I possibly could and left me in the library to get started.

When I awoke, I remembered the dream in detail, and still to this day, remember it like no other dream I've ever had. The motion of riding in the truck up to the building, seeing the other people helped out of the truck. Meeting God, and not being surprised or afraid. The admonition to study and learn.

That dream had a significant impact on me, and set me on a course of deliberate study, the kind of learning that comes from books, classrooms, and courses taken. I have also learned from mishaps, mistakes, and missteps. Then, there have been those life lessons learned from just living day to day, and being open to learning what lesson a particular experience held for me. Some of my learning has been through intention – scheduling a class, working on my master's, being a part of a group study – be it Bible study or a book study. Some of my learning has come through reflection and diving into what the meaning of a moment, instance or incident held for me.

This life mission of learning has brought me to a place of awareness. The kind of awareness that has me living my life with a thoughtfulness, intention, and purpose I have deliberately cultivated.

In 2008, I made the (what I know now to be a very bold) decision to leave my financially comfortable career as a financial advisor making six figures, with all sorts of perks: trips, awards, my own branch office and branch office administrator, social prestige, community esteem and the admiration of my husband as to the career I had built. What no one except my branch office administrator and my husband knew, however, was how completely miserable and physically ill I was in this career. Yes, I won the awards and the trips. Yes, I made incredible money, but at night I had the most gruesome insomnia one could imagine. I was plagued by migraines and poor health. My marriage was in the proverbial tank. I was a mess. I felt trapped and thought there was no way to rectify the horrible state I was in, other than quitting and leaving that career. I walked away feeling like a failure and carried that awfulness with me for quite some time. It wasn't until I met this woman at a conference and we were doing the whole 'this is my life, yada, yada, yada' conversation that I got a different twist on the decision I had made. The gal turned to me after I gave her a brief description of what had transpired and she asked me, "What gave you the strength and courage to do that?"

Strength and courage? It was one of those moments where I thought she was talking to someone behind or beside me. Me? Is quitting such a prestigious and money-making career courageous? Yep, she was talking to me, and that one moment changed my life. It brought back the dream. I took a timeout from life for a while and spent some quiet time going back to the admonition to learn and study. I read, I prayed, and I sought answers. I looked at my life and learned through forgiveness – for my ex-husband, the company I left, my husband, and myself. I studied *me* and learned what fills me with joy, and what dreams I have for my life. What I learned is that I am created for *service*, *helping*, and *healing*. This is my life's calling. This is what dream I have to live and bring to fruition.

This study brought me to the path I now travel with intention, with clarity, and with purposeful creation every day.

Walking on my path of service, helping and healing has led me to more study, more learning. The biggest learning I've done is learning about myself. I could write a Ph.D. dissertation on Judith, and some post-doc work too! I've learned that I have gifts, God-given gifts that are to benefit others, and I bring them to a state of health and wholeness, both physically and emotionally. I have learned to shift and create mindset – mine first and foremost, and then to coach others on how they can create theirs, too. I have learned to release trapped emotions and bring the body back to balance and homeostasis. I've learned about natural, holistic methods and modalities to deliver peace, happiness, and contentment to those I help.

When I started this lifestyle of natural, holistic healing by utilizing my gifts, little did I know the effect it would have on those around my family, friends, and me. I naively thought the work I was doing was mostly for my benefit and then tangentially for the benefit of my relationship with my husband and our marriage. I wasn't fully aware of the effect my shift was having on my children. I have since learned that I create my space and those around me naturally come into that space I have created. Thus, affecting them and causing shifts for them too.

This message of creation, space, and shift was brought home to me a couple of months ago. I would love to tell you it was an occurrence of rainbows, butterflies, and puppies. Alas, not so. As with most growth, it came with pain, heartache, and sorrow.

I went through a hellish time with my youngest daughter. It was the sort of stuff that parent's nightmares are made of. Kind of fitting with the dream theme of my life. My daughter moved to live and work on a ranch in Oklahoma and attend classes for her first semester of college. As the semester progressed, so did the verbal and emotional abuse the trainers heaped upon my daughter. She was living on their ranch and left in October. After couch surfing to the end of the semester, she returned home to attend the local junior college for her spring semester. Between semesters, she sustained a severe injury after getting bucked from a horse. Her knee was shot. The spring semester was shot too. Dropped classes, academic probation, and much stress ensued.

Then May hit, and I don't use the word hit lightly. It hit like a *storm*. My son was rear-ended, and his car was totaled. One of my other daughters went through relationship issues. My dad was hospitalized with the effects of dementia and Alzheimer's, and we were advised to place him in an Alzheimer's unit of a care facility. In addition to all this, my youngest daughter went through her own personal hell; and I went through hell with her. Without giving you all the gory details, which included much heartache, sleepless nights, long days and exceptionable stress, the calendar turned to June.

Our daughter moved out and went to live with a friend. She was cold and distant. I was in a fog. I couldn't understand how my precious girl was so off course. How could she have made such bad decisions? How could she turn her back on our family ethos of attending college? Where had I failed as a parent and failed her?

Slowly, we started communicating and talking about what had happened, and here's what it was... my daughter went through exactly what I went through in 2008. She was miserable and felt trapped in a situation from which she didn't know how to extricate herself. Without sufficient communication skills to convey her frustration with the situation, she suffered. I suffered. It was *tough*.

As I talked to her more and more and studied the situation, I realized that this precious daughter of mine had learned my lesson oh so well.

What lesson what that?

She felt the call to follow *her* dreams. Not my dreams, not the family's dreams. Hers. She learned that she has the ability to create life on her terms, her way.

As I mourned and went through the sadness of her decisions to not return to college and to move out, I had one of those lightning bolt moments where I woke up to the fact that I was mourning the loss of *my* dreams for her. Then, I found myself in a state of awe and wonder that the student (my daughter) became the teacher. It became apparent that she went through the same learning process and had the same experiences as me. She saw me make a stand for myself when I was miserable, unhappy, sick, and at the edge. When she was in that place in her life, she took a stand for herself. Communication styles differed and the end result was the same.

My 'ah-ha' moment was the shift for me. I shifted my view of what I went through from a place of heartache and pain to a place of pride that my daughter *got it*.

She got that she has her own dreams, and gets to live life on her terms. She chooses her path and creates her way. Just like I did.

Just like in the dream I had when I was in my early twenties where I was admonished to study and learn, I keep on doing so. I studied the hellish month I went through, and I learned that as a mother I can choose to surrender and release my kiddos to follow their path, with all the love I have for them. It's *so* much better for them and peaceful for me! I shift from the 'mother' role to friend and coach role. I had a great friend who lovingly told me, "You've done a great job raising them. They are great people." She's right. They are.

I know that this won't be the last life lesson for me by any means. The excitement lies in knowing that with every lesson, there is that rainbows, butterfly and puppies moment for me when I see with all clarity the gift of the lesson, and that's the best dream of all!

Kate Holt

Kate Holt RN, CCEP is the executive director of the Institute of Core Energetics, a speaker, trainer, and coach. As the owner of Holt Mentoring and Education Services, she works with transformation-industry entrepreneurs who want to make a profitable impact. Kate is passionate about helping people find the depth they long for in relationships, and to live their innate greatness out loud. She uses cutting-edge body-based technology, love, and humor, combined with her knack for zeroing in on what needs to shift next so they can build greater intimacy and make a bigger impact while maintaining their integrity.

Learn more about Kate:

Websites: www.kateholt.global

www.coreenergetics.org

https://kateholt.lpages.co/yourshiftmatters/

Chapter 14

I'll Have a Life of Pie

By Kate Holt

All the outer trappings were there. We had a beautiful home in the suburbs on an acre of land. The kids were in great schools and had seemingly adjusted to our new neighborhood. Everyone who was old enough to drive had a car in the driveway. He was making enough money that I no longer needed to work as a nurse. I was able to stay home with the kids. Perfect.

Sitting in the Diamond Diner, where we sometimes come to have a 'state of our family' kind of meeting, it's tense. I feel my body fighting against collapse, as I sense the distance between us growing wider. Everything hurts as I cling to this relationship that is difficult at best and is now dying. For ten years, we've been working too hard to keep it together. Still, I hold on desperately, which only serves to push him farther away. A voice in my head is screaming, 'You can't have a second failed marriage!' We both feel trapped. It's palpable.

Growing up, if I stomped up the stairs in anger, I was forced to come down and walk back up quietly. I was not allowed to say, "Shut up" or "I hate you." These natural negative expressions amidst family conflict were thwarted. Expressions of sexuality felt dangerous, too. The risk of shame and humiliation was too great.

In the fourth grade, my mother gave me the news. "Aunt Lydie died." I burst into tears, and she chastised me. "What are you crying for? People only do that for show." The implied message was, 'You can't trust what you feel'. When my father died, I was fourteen, and I could barely cry. Deep down I thought something must be terribly wrong with a girl who can't cry when her father dies.

It seemed that love and laughter were the only expressions that were fully permissible in my family. Humor became very precious. In some ways, laughter saved my sanity. It's no coincidence that I've always been super attracted to funny men or that I delight in making people laugh.

Keeping it all inside or finding a way to make it funny became my unconscious habits to stay safe, but how did I do that? I swallowed down hard on tears that came up, tightened my jaw to keep from screaming, made jokes and giggled to minimize hurt or humiliation, drank alcohol to manage powerful sexual feelings and my fear of intimacy. Suppression of emotions is physical, as well as psychological.

We bite back tears. We tighten shoulder muscles to keep from swinging the fist or legs muscles to keep from kicking. We freeze pelvic muscles to inhibit writhing in pleasure. To alleviate anxiety, we leak the energy that feels too intense.

Repressed feelings wreak havoc in any relationship. Long periods of held feelings led to physical pain and multiple unexplained ailments. When he would travel for business, my lack of trust and fear of abandonment would show up as physical illness. I got sick almost every time he went away; fevers, sore throats, stomach bugs, you name it. Inevitably, an emotional eruption would follow my prolonged withholding of anger and hurt. My volatility made it scary to be in a relationship with me.

I'm yelling at him, telling him how horrible he is, how I won't put up with this anymore. I want to stop, but I can't. I'm threatening to end the marriage, while simultaneously terrified that he will. I'm panicking because I know if I don't stop, he'll walk out the door, and he might not talk to me for days. That's the pattern, but I can't stop because maybe I'll say the one thing that will make him see me and my pain. Maybe I'll say just the right words to make him feel the compassion for me that I cannot feel for myself. I resolve to stop but my cruelty comes out, and I say things I can't take back. I keep yelling and when the door slams, I cry. I cry until I can't cry anymore. When he comes back, he freezes me out. My apologies fall on deaf ears. I feel like I'll die. It's unbearable. Time passes so slowly in the frozen tundra. Eventually something shifts, we melt. Then we try again, go to counseling, sail along until the next time the pattern repeats. It's hell, but I can't bear another breakup... or so I think.

It almost feels like I'm talking about someone else. The 'me' I am describing was a personality constructed over many years to survive and cope with profound loss, loneliness, and insecurity. A substitute self, full of control patterns, hid my true essence; a living mask that no longer serves the purpose of protecting me. It has instead become the source of my pain.

I was pretty good at talking about my feelings, but not really feeling them. A colleague of mine addresses the difference this way: talking about feelings is like reading a recipe for apple pie. Feeling them is like actually eating the pie.

On the outside, I appeared outgoing, funny, confident but also judgmental and sometimes arrogant. I tried very hard to be a good mom. I wanted to be a good wife, but I was deeply resistant to complying with any 'good wife' standards. I seemed to perceive everything as a demand. Even normal expectations felt like too much. I was trying to give from a system that was depleted, and I wondered why nothing was working.

I kept seeking answers. I frequented the self-help section, hoping Oprah would have the key. I decided to study hypnosis. It had worked for smoking cessation; I thought it might help again. In fact, it opened my mind and led to my interest in holistic approaches. I knew the pain in my body was connected to my emotional intensity and lack of control. I was riddled with tension in my back, jaw, neck, and shoulders. I desperately wanted to heal my body, change my behavior, and learn to be happy. I desperately wanted to love and be loved.

Late one night, I was reading about how we hold emotions in our bodies, in Barbara Brennan's book, *Hands of Light*. I turned the page to an illustration that stopped me in my tracks. It was a depiction of a woman with her back arched over a roller in a Core Energetics session. There was gray energy being released from the front of her body. I could feel my back and chest tighten. It was as if the drawing was speaking to me on a visceral level. Whatever this was, I needed it.

At the diner, he says he doesn't want to set up date nights anymore; it feels like too much pressure. "But we never did anything for our 10th anniversary," I protest. He doesn't want to. Suddenly, I feel so alone. As much as we've struggled and fought, I always felt his commitment to trying to make it work. This time it's different. It's ending. I can feel it.

I found a Core Energetics practitioner and quickly discovered it was a safe way for me to release what was pent-up in me for a lifetime. My practitioner received my feelings without judgment. She seemed to know exactly how to elicit them through simple movements, subtle adjustments to my posture, and by asking gentle but provocative questions. I started to uncover the source of my negative patterns. Even though I sensed our marriage ending, there was a flicker of hope when I touched my core essence that let me know I'd be okay. When it did end, it felt like my Core Energetics work was too little, too late. If only I could have started this work sooner!

However, I persisted. My devastation shattered my defensives along with my arrogance. I was literally brought to my knees in surrender to God. I made a humble prayer, unlike my usual prayers of petition, begging for life to be different. I prayed to see myself clearly and compassionately. I prayed to change. I asked God to save me from what felt like my demise. "I can't do it alone!" The Serenity Prayer became my mantra. "God grant me the serenity to accept the things I cannot change, the courage to change the things I can and the wisdom to know the difference."

Hardened tensions unraveled in my body and I began to release years of grief, tears, fits of rage, and unspoken protests. After each session, I was softer, more open. My rigid beliefs softened too.

Mid-session, after some directed movement, my legs start to vibrate. Involuntary tremors move up through my body. At first, it's painful as the wave meets tension and resistance in my belly and chest. She encourages me to vocalize with soft sounds. Then I hear this wailing, a voice I don't recognize. Suddenly, I realize it's coming from me. It's the voice of a soul longing to be born. It's my soul reincarnating in this life. After a few minutes, the vibrations become finer, pleasurable. An incredible sense of calm washes over me. Fear and insecurity have vanished. I'm deeply affected, born anew.

The work isn't only about the emotional release though. It's also about owning and transforming my negativity, seeing previously hidden aspects of myself. It's about learning to bring my voice and to put my strong will in service of my heart, as opposed to my ego. It's about learning to fill my depleted system from within, so

I have more to give. It's about learning to trust and show my vulnerability.

In order to mature and develop spiritually and emotionally, we need access to all of our emotions. What we repress is always seeking expression, and it will find a way to leak out. As the saying goes, 'You need to feel it to heal it'. We also need to take responsibility for the forces operating within us, by bringing them into the light of consciousness.

This is what gives you access to your core and your true capacity for love. You can't do it alone. You need someone to guide you, someone who's gone down that path and done their work. Core Energetics touched me so deeply. It reacquainted me with my core essence. The process was hard work, and it took time, but it was worth every penny, every minute, and every bit of effort. I went from being shut down to having full access to my heart. I went from volatile to contained, from arrogant to humble. I went from wanting to love, to actually loving. I developed my emotional and relational intelligence. I became a better, less controlling mother, a better friend. I became more comfortable with my sexuality, resolving years of Catholic shame. I began to live more abundantly and to experience life as a playground of possibilities.

I wrote this poem as a reflection of some deep work I had done in sessions:

Note to Self: Permission Opens all the Possibilities.

The only place to go when demand attempts to smother, is away.

Away from you, away from love, away from ok, away from 'Yes, I will'.

The righteousness you swallowed to stave off your imaginary demise, betrayed you.

Betrayed your spontaneous soul movement, betrayed all your potential truth.

The real you sits there under the sludge of 'Be good' and 'No, No, No' and 'Shhhhh'.

The day comes when you grumble under your breath,

'If I have to swallow any more, I'll explode!'

But, somehow, you manage to eat more poison, grudgingly.

It really hurts…it's hard to breathe, move, feel…you fantasize of dying to escape the morass.

.From under the muck, the longing for freedom bubbles up and utters a fervent prayer but still you suffer.

Then one day the mystical ipecac is introduced…you sip cautiously at first.

Thankfully, the shaman has a cushion and a bucket and holds back your hair.

You hurl out the rage, heave out the grief, in growls and wails and whimpers…it is a long dark night.

And in the morning, you sip the cool water of self-declared permission and feel a 'Maybe'.

Though our marriage ended, the Core Energetics work helped me relate better through the divorce and beyond. We found a stride in cooperative parenting that served our children well. Years later, we have a truly loving relationship, one in which our children and grandchildren see us get along and collaborate for the good of our family.

After two years doing sessions, I entered the Institute of Core Energetics' four-year practitioner training. Engaging with such a deeply committed group of people was profoundly life-changing. It was the most transformational period of my life. For a while I balanced my nursing career with a private practice in Core Energetics, working with individuals, groups, and couples. Eventually, I left nursing and found ways to integrate the work with business coaching. My passion is training and supervising practitioners to help them discover their unique style and gifts and to help them reach more people with this sacred work of reclamation. Helping others develop their personal power and relational intelligence has implications for the world. The ripple effect of each person accessing and living from their core essence has the power to positively impact families, organizations, communities, and nations.

Sixty-five-year-old, Bill (not his real name) has had a lifetime of difficulty in personal and professional relationships. He's been working with me for several months. He says, "The most amazing thing happened this week. I was in a meeting with a business contact who challenged me, pretty aggressively. I responded in such a different way than I would have in the past. Instead of getting defensive or pushing my point of view, I simply listened. I was able to hear the truth of his concern. I didn't have to think about the right way to respond, it just went well. I was honest and rational. He calmed down, and we were able to move the conversation forward, where we typically would've reached an impasse. I'm so glad, because this guy matters to me, and so does the work we're doing. I realized, I am changing from the inside and out and it feels great."

I love what this work did for me and what it does for my clients. While there are cognitive components, it's not about teaching them techniques or how to think. They show up, and the work changes them organically and their lives expand. Their relationships improve. They become empowered.

Eighteen years and many leadership lessons after starting the training, I now head up the Institute of Core Energetics. I sense that I was always meant to do exactly this. I have amazingly supportive relationships there and in my personal life. I'm known for my abiding calm presence, stamina, and my ability to hold space for intense emotions and conflicts, so they can resolve. I'm living the life I was born to live.

Klara Gubacs-Collins

Like you, winning mindset expert and author Dr. Klara Gubacs-Collins has seen the phrase 'winning mindset' defined numerous ways. Is it positive thinking or confidence? Is it meant only for the chosen few? Or is it for all who applies the proper principles in the right sequence?

She defines a winning mindset as the quiet confidence resulting from effectively combining physical, mental, and emotional skills. Dr. Gubacs-Collins' expertise stems from years of studies and multiple championships in many sports. She teaches a unique blend of skills to bring students and clients from contender to champion in sports, business, and life.

Learn more about Klara:

Website: www.winningmindinstitute.com

Email: dr.gubacs@winningmindtherapy.com

Twitter: https://twitter.com/chump2champfast

Chapter 15

Contender to Champion: Discovering Your Zone of Genius

By Klara Gubacs-Collins

It is 1978, when a little girl, who was supposed to be a boy, is asked by her all male playing buddies, "Can you come out to play?" She says, "I just need to finish the dishes and I will be out there, promise!" That's how every day went in this girl's life – as she snuck away day in and day out to play soccer with her male buddies. "Look I just learned the new Maradona move," she would yell, as she went into her dream of becoming a famous 'male' soccer player! But as she grew older – one day – to her utter desperation, she found that she would be a girl after all! No more AC Milan contract! No more Hungarian national soccer team! Damn it, she is a woman with a stupid period! Why? Eyewitnesses explain the hysterical breakdown this girl had when she learned there was no turning back!

But wait! There is hope! Let's master tennis! She is just like Steffi Graf! She can be on the Hungarian national team and go to the Olympics as a tennis superstar! She practiced hitting tennis balls on any wall, including the wall of their house, at her father's dismay as the paint was crumbling down! She was going to be an Olympian! Then a decision was made by people that loved her very much, albeit at that time it didn't seem like it! She learned from her parents that she would not be an Olympian, at least not in tennis.

Fast-forward to 2008, when this girl, me, picked up in another sport (golf) that I thought would take me to winning the Hungarian national championship; finally earning my ticket to the Olympics to represent Hungary in Rio! But instead of glory, the clouds of a perfect storm gathered fast in my life with three significant life events as its main elements.

First, in 2013 I started to get sick. As a usually healthy person, I thought that it would pass, but I became lethargic, moody and forgetful. As my husband so eloquently described it, I was PMSing 24/7; he was right. To make it even worse I started to gain weight for no reason. I have always been a rather predictable person regarding my diet, and I knew I did not change anything. The fatigue also coupled with body pains finally sent me to the doctor.

I was diagnosed with hypothyroidism and was told that I need to take pills for about two months and that if they didn't help I may need surgery. Since some family members have been treated for thyroid disease, it seemed plausible. From my years of studies, I also learned that genetics only determine a very small percentage of health issues, so I set out to search for my own answers. I found that undiagnosed food allergies could exhibit the same symptoms, and maybe even become the cause of thyroid problems. Learning from my physician father, I went on a strict food elimination diet. Within weeks, I learned which foods I should never eat again. Then I contacted a naturopathic doctor and we went on to heal my gut and bring me back to a better physical condition than ever. It took over six months of eliminating dairy, wheat (including my favorite, beer), and grains from my diet, but it was all worth it.

However, this health problem became a significant element of the perfect storm as it blocked me from clear thinking and made my days miserable. I didn't want to wake-up in the morning and certainly didn't want to go to work. Oh yes, work. The issues at work became the second element of my perfect storm. I truly loved my profession as a teacher and university professor, but because of my declining health and the changes in the institution's policies, I could not find pleasure in my work anymore. I loved my profession but hated my job.

Then came the last straw. Until then I could always find solace in my sports. I could just go hit or kick some balls around and feel great, but that highway to success also began to crumble. As a lifelong athlete, I knew what I had to do to 'make it' in my new sport. From 2009 to 2014, I tried so hard to play better golf so I could be a champion at my club, a dream I had for years. Why? Because I realized that the real Olympics might not happen for me, so I made the club championship my 'Olympics'. With that win, I would have accomplished what I termed a 'career grand slam' as by then I won the tennis, platform tennis and both golf championships in the same club. A feat no man or woman would have ever done.

I went on to practice for an inordinate amount of time. I clipped the golf masters and their messages out of all the golf magazines. I was putting together what I thought was 'the winning strategy', all to no avail. I kept choking. I was trying to be a great golfer, but I sabotaged being the great athlete that I was from birth.

So, let me recount my life at this point. I was blaming the university for changing on me. I was blaming my coaches in the sports for my failing. I blamed genetics for my health issues. I was a victim of all my circumstances crumbling down fast while being told by the people that loved me to give up trying for the championship. However, I am not a quitter, and as I solved the problem with my health, I decided to find the solution for my lack of performance in 'perceived' pressure situations. After years of studies in energy psychology and inner reconciliation, I found the answer.

In the spring of 2015, I designed the winning mind blueprint that allowed me to reconcile with myself and my style of playing and persona in life. I reconciled with the possibility that I may never be a consistent enough golfer to take on Goliath and that I may never win the championship. That summer I went into the competition with complete surrender and qualified for the finals, where on the last, the 27th hole, I won. I kept surrendering after every good and not so good shot. I never got excited or sad, and never lost the focus of the purpose of the game. The purpose, in this case, was not to prove how great I was or how beautiful my swing was but to get the ball in the hole the fastest possible way.

I recognized during my misery that wanting to be 'someone' else, in my case, a golfer, didn't allow me to be me – the athlete. By wanting to be someone else, I blocked my genius from coming to the surface and carrying me to success. The biggest shift you can make in your life happens when you stop fighting who you are mentally, physically, and emotionally. You are created perfectly with all that you may deem faults or weaknesses. Every characteristic that sets you apart from others are your calling cards, what makes you unique. The moment you accept that you are not as good as others in an area of life, it will allow you to let that part go and focus on your unique ability that makes you stand out. Every one of us has what I term a zone of genius. You need to find your zone of genius and build your life on that while you completely accept every other part of you. Below I will share some practical examples of how I, and hopefully you, can find your zone of genius in our sometimes competitive world.

I read in many books that you are supposed to 'grow out' of being the competitor if you are heading 'properly' toward your evolution. I tried, boy did I try to be compassionate and understanding on the golf course and on the tennis court, and you know what happened? While I was compassionate, I was being beaten by people that understood why they were on the court and course. While I was giving tips for my opponents to get better, they rose to the occasion to beat me. No, you don't need to change who you are, but you must cater to all aspects of you in its proper venue. I still give tips because that is the teacher in me, but I also compete to see whether my opponent or I will be the one that uses the tip more efficiently.

So am I a teacher *and* a coach? Yes, and I will continue to take my absolute best every single day into the classroom or into my online coaching. Am I a caretaker? Most definitely, and I will continue to care for my mother and my husband who needs my attention.

Am I also a competitor? You had better believe it! Being competitive on the playing field where competition is called for is not bad – it's required! The only question is whether you can act accordingly in every situation. If competition is called for, then *compete*. If cooperation is required, then *cooperate*. Your life takes its shape in many situations and you must learn to behave accordingly in each.

You should learn who you are by at least midlife for goodness sake! When you've learned, accept it and use it to propel you in the direction you want to go in each area of your life! Compartmentalize, because you can! You can be the most compassionate mother but a tough opponent to your fellow lawyer in the courtroom! Don't make my mistake for years! Work for what you need to, compete for your wins and care for the people that are in need!

I spent years trying to eliminate the physical and emotional pain that was surfacing throughout my perfect storm. I read hundreds of self-help and motivational literature. I took dozens of online courses and certification programs to learn to eliminate feeling bad, sad or hurt. However, it was not until very recently did I realize that it's not about fighting with your physical or emotional pain! It's about letting them come to you in a quiet conversation, so they let you know what they need! Even if you are the strongest athlete, you hurt for a reason. Or if you have emotional pain it wants to be understood! Don't try to eliminate it! *Understand* it!

What would you do if a child that was just bullied came to you crying? Would you tell them to fight the feeling inside, or would you tell them to explain what hurt and why it felt bad? Sometimes life will bully you! Why can't you sit down with yourself and discuss the pain instead of learning to hate the bully, or even worse, hate yourself for letting it happen! I was bullied this year in competition, and it hurt but had no time until later – when I lost – to talk to myself and see why I was hurting! However, once me, myself and Klara discussed the pain, it magically disappeared! I don't hate my opponent, and I don't hate myself for not recognizing the pain of being bullied! Let life in! When pain comes don't fight it, describe it and do it in some detail! You will learn about yourself not only how to act now but how to strengthen yourself for the future!

Consequently, I experienced the biggest turning point in my life when I stopped looking for myself, outside of myself. For example, when I stopped seeking spiritual awakening and understood that I am as 'awake' as I can be at this very moment. I don't have to follow a spiritual guru to know who I'm supposed to be because I already *am* me. Can I listen to others and grow? Of course I can since that is what going through life is all about. However, I don't have to make my growth contingent upon learning something new. I make it by accepting that by existing another minute, and another day on this earth I *will* grow. Just like wildflowers, if nourished by nature can't be stopped from growing. You are just the same. If you allow nature to guide you toward your direction, and give up trying to control your every single step, it's the only way you will reach your true destination.

The main step is to accept that how an event affects you is the right response from you in that very minute. Why? Because that is the 'only' response you are capable of at that moment. If you got angry instead of loving, so be it. You learn from the situation and let life move you to the next step. The constant fight to be 'better' or more 'loving' is exhausting and that exhaustion stops you from living your life in the moment. By *trying* to be a champion, by *trying* to be a better teacher, by *trying* to be a better person I lost my chance to fully experience life for many years. This will be detrimental in your marriage and in your business life just the same. If you are not authentic in your business, people will find out fast. Don't try to be someone – *let yourself be you.* If you are in it for the money or the service or whatever is your motivation, say so! You will get much further ahead, I can promise you that now.

If you liked this message, then do yourself a favor; before you move into the next chapter get a piece of paper or even your phone or tablet and write down *every single thing* that you want to do in life that would challenge you to accept who you are! Design a mind map around it and write up the exact steps you would need to take in the next one to six months to fulfill your zone of genius. Then achieve - or at least make major steps toward - the direction of your Olympics! Share it with me if you wish and let me help you get to it! There has never been a better feeling in my life than when I got into college against all the odds, or when I received my doctorate and finally, when I won 'my Olympics'! Almost no one believed that I would do it! Almost no one will believe in you either! However, you and I will! Let's get you to at least to contend and then go from contender to champion in your business, sports, and life!

Lesha Kitts

Lesha Kitts answered her calling to be a healer at a very young age. She graduated from the NM School of Natural Therapeutics in 1987 and continued developing her skills as a healer. Due to a life threatening battle with cancer, she recognizes the importance of spiritual connection. Through her training as a certified natural therapeutics specialist, a certified spiritual practitioner, and her own life experiences, she was led to energy healing. As an energy healer she clears emotional blockages, releases physical trauma and ignites the light that dwells within to lead a happy, healthy, 'soular-powered' life!

Learn more about Lesha:

Website: www.SoularPoweredXSolPurpose.com

Email: SoularPoweredXSolPurpose@gmail.com

LeshaKitts@gmail.com

Chapter 16

Getting 'Tuned' In

By Lesha Kitts

I'd been working the same job for the last seven years. Same hours. Same location. Then one day the mother of a childhood friend walked in. "Lesha!' she exclaimed, "it is so good to see you. Shannon is in town, and I'm sure he would love to see you."

I quickly scribbled my phone number on a piece of paper and passed it across the counter. "I haven't seen Shannon since we were kids!" I replied. "Tell him to call me, and we'll catch up." Before my shift was over, he had called, and we made arrangements to meet at a local restaurant after work.

I arrived early at the notorious New Mexico restaurant, known for its southwestern cuisine and the fact that it can seat about fifteen hundred people. Needless to say, the parking lot is massive, but after ten minutes of looking for a parking space and unable to find one, I chalked it up to the fact that it just wasn't meant to be. I called Shannon to inform him that there wasn't a parking space to be had. He promptly suggested another restaurant the next town over. I was tired. I didn't really want to go, but something made me agree to it, and the next thing I knew, I was on the road to Bernalillo.

We sat at the bar and ordered drinks. A short time later, a band showed up to play. The singer was in eyeshot, just over Shannon's shoulder. She had a presence that draws you in. She was voluptuous and carried her head high with dignity. You could tell she was a strong woman. Life lessons experienced to their full potential created an enticing humbleness about her. She enraptured the room. She exuded sassiness, which was tempered by a kind, gentle underlying confidence.

Then she opened her mouth to sing. I *love* music, but I have *never* experienced such a powerhouse voice. While I have heard that there are people that are touched by Divine gift, this was the first time I'd ever gazed upon it, and I mean that literally. As the first resonant note drifted from her lips, I saw a luminous light ascend over her. I was in awe. I couldn't believe what I was *seeing*. I couldn't believe what I was *hearing*. A voice that can stir every emotion you ever dreamed of. It leads you to experience them in the very deepest part of your soul, in the moment of a perfectly held note. I was so touched by her voice that I left that night and never caught her name. I drove home with reminiscent tunes in my head of songs that she had sung and I thought to myself, *I should call tomorrow and find out who she is.*

That line ran through my mind many times over the next few months. Her voice would just pop into my head when my spirit needed to be uplifted. It soothed and comforted me. I felt safe and warm and in tune to life, but for some reason, I never called to find out who she was.

Four months later, I'm sitting in my doctor's office waiting for the results of a lumpectomy. Then came the words that no one wants to hear. "You have stage three breast cancer."

There must be some mistake. I'm only thirty-eight. I'm the athlete of the family. My credo is natural therapies and eating healthy. I am as strong as an ox. This can't be happening to me. The fear creeps in, and my walls go up. From this place of horrid apprehension, I cannot hear the voice of comfort sing to me this day.

However, the voice of reason *is* with me. My stepmother, Maggi, stands by my side as I receive this news and gently guides me in the process of decision-making. She is at every chemo session, radiation treatment, surgery, blood test, injection and supports me in any way I need. She is my rock that I lean on, and I will forever be grateful for her graceful presences in my life.

From the moment I am diagnosed, I became a medical pincushion. In the first week, I have numerous blood tests, an EKG, ECG, MRI, and other various things I can't begin to pronounce. When diagnosed, the plan is to have a double mastectomy the following Monday. After a week of poking, prodding, and testing, I finally meet my oncologist for the first time on Friday. She says that, due to the test results, we are going to start chemo on Monday instead of doing surgery. I have prepared my mind for surgery, and I am OK with that, but chemo on Monday? My mind panics. I thought I'd have more time to prepare. Just the word scares me. You see, my mother had passed away of a brain tumor when I was twenty, and she was only forty-four. I had been her caretaker in that year-long process. She was my best friend. The one I looked up to and wanted to be like. Now facing my own cancer, what my young mind remembered about this event was all of her friends saying, "Oh thank God she didn't have to have chemo!" Now this phrase echoes in my head and I am scared.

I go to work on Saturday. One of my customers – who has been going through cancer herself – comes in. She reminds me of my mother in how she handles her circumstances. Her attitude is amazingly positive. She comes in with her makeup all done, wearing a purple leather blazer and a headscarf with a cute hat tilted to one side, but *never* a wig. She doesn't want to hide her cancer. She wanted to show that you can be beautiful while going through something ugly. I admire her greatly. I ask my co-workers if I can sit down and talk to Jeannie. I haven't told her of my diagnosis. My co-workers are very supportive. They all know what she has been going through and admire her as much as I do. They know her words will help.

"Jeannie, I was just diagnosed with breast cancer this week. I start chemo on Monday. And I am really scared." Then my tears start to flow. It's the first time I am admitting that I am scared. My way of dealing with things is to get through it. Vulnerability to me is a weakness, and now here I sit, discovering it is one of the most powerful attributes of the human character that one may possess. The immense power of it kicks in as Jeannie reaches across the table and takes my hand. Through her loving touch and the following words of wisdom, my viewpoint and attitude is changed. "Oh Honey. Don't you worry. You have to think of chemo as your friend. We accept our friends for their good and their bad, but they are our friends because we focus on the *good*. Let chemo do what it *can* for you. And know that you are strong enough to get through what it *does* to you."

It's Monday morning, and I'm ready. Bob, my father and my foundation of strength, waits outside the room. His loving vigilance cradles me. My stepmother is by my side. As I sit in a comfy recliner, and the nurse searches for a vein in my arm, I'm thinking to myself, *It's only an hour. I can get through anything for an hour.* Maggi has brought magazines to distract us from what is about to happen. In the back of both of our minds is the reality that they are about to pump poison into my body. But she is steadfast and calm while I am focused on staying positive and not letting fear get the best of me.

The nurse finds a good vein, makes the line connection, starts the drip, and turns to walk away. I had *no* idea that blood travels that quickly through your body. My heart rate goes from normal to hummingbird in a split second. The nurse hadn't taken three steps away from me. I feel like I am being squeezed like a balloon. My face immediately flushes, and my head feels as if it is going to explode. I look at Maggi, and she looks back at me with panic. She reaches for my hand and says, "Are you OK?" All I could say is, "Get her!" In Maggi's authoritative teacher voice, all she needed was one word, "Nurse!" She turns, sees me and quickly grabs the line to stop the drip. Immediately I am surrounded by nurses and crash carts. I go into shock. My mind crumbles. *I'm going to die.* I'm thinking to myself. *My body just instantaneously rejected what could kill the cancer cells in my body. I'm going to die.*

I wait about twenty minutes for my oncologist to come in. While I sit in the comfy recliner, still hooked up to the chemo with the drip turned off, she squats down in front me and looks me in the eye. In a calming tone, she says, "I know that was scary for you. It is not uncommon, and we will deal with it. We're going to give you some Benadryl so your body will be more accepting of the chemo. We will be slowing the drip immensely, so your treatments will take eight or nine hours each time, instead of one or two."

My mind races. *Are you crazy? Eight or nine hours? I am only worried about the next few seconds!* I have never felt such sheer terror! I can choose to refuse it all and die of cancer, or I can allow them to try again and quite possibly die instantaneously! *I* am the only one that *experienced* what that crap did to me in a half second! I feel scared, overwhelmed and cornered. Maggi sits holding my hand to reassure me that I am not alone, but she knows the decision will have to be mine. I can't believe what I hear myself say, but for me, looking back, it was the only answer that could've been. I am a fighter. Not a quitter. So in this caged moment, I open myself to the power of vulnerability and trust for the first time in my life. "Ok. Let's do this."

I close my eyes, let go and say to myself, *Just let me get through this.* Before the echo of these words stop reverberating, that beautiful, comforting voice starts singing in my head… but this time it's different. They are songs I've never heard and they keep my mind in a peaceful, tranquil place. The voice sings in my head for the duration of my treatment as well as the next fifteen chemo treatments I receive. Eight to nine hours each time. This beautiful voice holds me in a healing space. I can't explain it. All I know is that I experienced her four months prior so that I may receive this gift right now. I have to trust in something in order to take down the wall and accept it. Cancer has a way of backing one into a corner, and it is forcing me to try on a new mindset to save my own life.

I have just been struck by Divine Spirits tuning fork. It is getting me tuning into the fact that we're all connected. I believe in Divine Spirit. I believe that we're all manifest from it. I believe that we're all individual expressions of it. This tells me we are all connected, and I am not alone, now or ever.

Six months later, the connection continues. I'm finally done with chemo and preparing for surgery. It is scheduled for the day after Easter. I tell my folks I'd like to attend Easter service to feel centered in preparation for surgery. It is a packed house. Upon entering the sanctuary, I am handed a program, and I take my seat. As my eyes scroll over the program, I hear a voice singing. Not just any voice. *The* voice. This time it isn't in my head. I lift my eyes to see where it was coming from. All I see is the slew of people and a light emanating from the podium. As the sea of heads parts, there stands the comforting voice that has saved my life. She is, on this sacred day, the guest musician at the spiritual center I have grown-up in. Her name is Hillary Smith. Had I not been buried in my work for the last ten years, I would've known her name. She is one of the most renowned singer/songwriters in New Mexico. Her lists of accolades are as long as my arm. So, where have I been? My tears flow as deep gratitude washes over me.

In a soft, sentimental intonation and tear-filled eyes, I approach her, "You don't know who I am, but I know your voice, and it saved my life." With her beautiful little girl, Lyric Lorraine, gazing up at her in admiration, I tell the story of how her voice had carried me through chemo. Then this radiant being of light takes my hands in hers, looks deeply and genuinely into my eyes, and filled with grace, she says, "You are going to be OK." I believe her. I feel a heart connection and the power of that connection to all that is. She is right. I am OK.

Now I call myself, 'The Soular Powered Sol'. Each and every day I practice opening to my connection with others and releasing trapped emotions that restrict life from being experienced to its fullest potential. The gratitude that I feel for the lessons learned through this tragic event are immense. The wisdom that Jeannie shared in dealing with her cancer. The unwavering support of my stepmother, Maggi, who has become a mother to me. The foundation of strength of mind that I inherited from my father, Bob. We are exactly the same, strong and true. I know this now, and I am honored to be his daughter. The foresight of my loving brother Curtis, as he kept my dreams of a future alive, never letting negative thoughts destroy my heart and soul. Hillary Smith for teaching me what it truly looks like to express the gifts that spirit has given you and Divine Spirit for orchestrating this life lesson.

Vulnerability is what allows us to open our hearts and experience our connection to others. It allows us to be and live from a place that is raw, real and worth the risk.

Your gifts are the ones that stand before you. Open them up! Then open up *to* them, for you are a gift to them as well. The bond of a vulnerable heart connection is the strongest I have ever experienced. Get tuned in, connect and live as the light that you are! Namaste.

Lois Wilson

Lois Wilson is an author, artist, storyteller, teacher, musician and spiritual guide; as well as the mother of five intrepid young adults. Her work and life are one. She acquired the love and wisdom she freely shares by living a messy, gorgeous, fearless, spirit-led life; while going straight through the middle of things, falling, getting the wind knocked out of her, and getting back up again! Lois holds three master's degrees (in theology, divinity, and education) and a Doctorate in Art and Spirituality. She is grateful to be still learning and growing every day.

Learn more about Lois:

Website: www.loiswilson.org

Facebook: Facebook.com/DrLoisWilson

Email: DrLoisWilson@gmail.com

Chapter 17

Who's Gonna Have the Last Word?

By Lois Wilson

I have one of those dates.

The dates that divide your life neatly in half, and not in a good way.

Forever after, you see your life in two parts: everything that happened before that date, and everything that happens after. Life as you once knew it is never, ever the same.

The events behind the creation of these dates differ. It could be a diagnosis. It could be a phone call from a hospital, police station or morgue. It could be a note hastily scrawled and left on a table or by the bed. It could be many things, and the details vary, but what these dates hold in common is the undeniable fact that *without* invitation or warning, your life is suddenly and irrevocably changed.

My date is March 3, 1999. After months of developmental testing, I sat in a tiny room at The Center for Autism in Philadelphia, Pennsylvania, filled with dread. "Elijah has infantile autism," Dr. Ruttenberg, The Center's founder said, as kindly as he possibly could.

The bottom of my world dropped out. Dr. Ruttenberg kept speaking, but I couldn't hear him. It was as though I was suddenly plunged underwater... my limbs were numb; I couldn't move, my mind couldn't grasp what I was hearing. I was sinking into a deep dark hole. A hole where I lived for the next two years, alone.

Elijah... my darling, adored, two-year-old son... the youngest of a noisy tribe of five... had autism. In 1999, autism was diagnosed at the rate of one in 110,000 children. Most people didn't know anyone with autism. If you told someone that your child was 'autistic' they smiled and thought you *meant* to say 'artistic' and asked you what kind of art: painting, dancing, music...theater?

In 1999, there were no online support groups, no fundraising walks, no 'autism awareness', no 'autism acceptance' campaigns, and no *I Love Someone with Autism* t-shirts, buttons, baseball caps, or bags.

I went home from The Center that day numb and dazed. The next morning I drove to Barnes and Noble in a fog of grief. I stumbled over to the section of books labeled *Special Needs Children* and found six books about autism – none of which were written for parents. I pulled all six down off the shelf, sat on the floor, read them... and cried.

Prior to March 3, 1999, I had one image in my mind associated with autism, thanks to a course in developmental psychology I took as an undergraduate at Penn State in 1978. Alongside my fellow classmates in the College of Human Development, I viewed a black and white filmstrip of a child in a catatonic state, rocking, moaning, and banging his head against a wall. That was autism. That was all I knew.

I got up off the floor and walked to the counter to purchase the three books I thought might be most helpful. Thus began what I came to refer to as 'The Education I Never Wanted'. I became an expert in autism because I had no other choice.

For two years, I cried every day. I never knew when the tears would start; I just knew that they *would*. I wondered what I had ever cried about before. I wondered if I would ever laugh again.

I also wondered why autism felt like such a *personal* assault. Why did this particular disorder feel so deeply and *personally* devastating? The answer came one afternoon while reading a book by a child psychologist describing the basis of the diagnosis: autism is defined by a severe disability in one's ability to empathize with others, coupled with a severe disability in one's ability to communicate with others.

There it was. Autism shattered the two things that made my life rich and meaningful – empathy and communication. My precious two-year-old son lived in a world I could not access. I wondered every day if he would ever know how much I loved him.

Grief became my constant companion. Relief came only when I fell asleep at night. The worst moment of every day came first thing each morning when I began to rise from a dream state into consciousness, floating upwards, only to be met again with the unbearable weight of my son's diagnosis greeting me just as I reached the surface.

For the first time in my life, this resourceful, stubborn, resilient Taurus was up against something I could not change, could not *will* my way through, and could not alter even one little bit. Accepting the situation was the only thing I could do... and I couldn't do it.

I was *furious* at God. I threw my Bible against the wall until the spine broke. I screamed at God until I lost my voice. I told God to do things that are anatomically impossible for God to do.

In my anguish and anger, I both swore at and prayed to the God I hated and loved, rejected and needed, cursed and implored.

I was working my way through my pain...but I didn't know it at the time.

What I was learning was that God was not afraid of my anguish, not offended by my profanity, not exhausted by my grief. God hung in there with me. When I occasionally wore myself out to the point where I reached a moment of silence, I could *almost* hear God breathing, her heart beating, her tears falling just like mine.

There was no short cut. I would have welcomed one, more than anything, but no. This was a long road with two companions: grief (who I feared) on one side, and God (who I hated) on the other. Patient, tireless, immovable companions, and no shortcut in sight.

Two years passed. We found a developmental pediatrician and a neurologist (fun fact: children with autism are far more likely to have grand mal seizures than typically developing children). We found a speech therapist and an occupational therapist who came to our home every week to work with Eli and who became part of the family. We enrolled Eli in the preschool program at The Center for Autism, and we were assigned a leader for Eli's treatment team: a young psychologist, Dr. Eric Mitchell.

Eric came to our home once a week. He spent time with *all* of us... Eli, my tribe of children, my husband, and me. I would sit at the kitchen table, and he would listen with infinite compassion as I wept. He gave me words that were like small floating rafts in a sea of pain, and he asked me questions. Good questions. Painful questions. Lifesaving questions.

The turning point came one ordinary Wednesday afternoon. I remember the Kleenex box near me on the table while we talked.

I remember my noisy tribe building forts in the living room with the sofa cushions.

"Lois, are you going to let autism have the last word?" Eric asked.

My mind stopped still. From deep, deep down inside of me, for the first time in two years, I realized I *did* have a choice.

I didn't have a choice of whether or not Eli had autism (he did), nor how severe it would be (very severe), but I *did* have a choice regarding *how much power* autism had over my life.

I could choose to have the last word.

I am not going to tell you that everything changed all at once that afternoon. What I am going to tell you is that something *shifted in me,* and a brand new trajectory was established. I decided that autism would *not* have the last word in my life. I decided that *I* would determine what this experience meant, how I would respond to it, and where I (and my family) would go from here.

Grief was still walking with me every single day, but so was hope; I hadn't seen her in a long, long time.

What followed were *years* of radical self-care, a slow re-emergence of my willingness to trust God (only a little at first, and then a bit more) and learning how to reframe my experiences in a way that fed my ever-so-tiny sense of hope that I (and my family) would somehow survive.

As I said earlier, it doesn't really matter *what* catapults you into the land of 'Life Will Never Ever Be the Same'. Your details will be different from mine, but our pathways are the same, through and through. Here are my words of guidance for you:

Feel your feelings. Don't try to gloss over them, hide them, decorate them or fix them. Embrace and express them in all their profane glory. This will take time, and it will be exhausting. Don't listen to anyone who tells you it's too much or you should be over it by now... They may mean well, but they're feeling scared and helpless, and they don't understand. Let God be the dumping ground (She can take whatever you dish out) and any other trusted soul with a loving heart and nerves of steel because they're gonna need both.

Befriend grief. What you are experiencing, regardless of the details, is *loss*. Face it. Name it. I lost the child I thought I would raise, the family I thought I would have, the future I expected for myself, for Eli, and for his four older siblings. I lost my confidence as a mother. I lost my peace, my joy, and my hope. I lost my faith in God and in the safety of life itself. Make your list. Grieve it all.

Take a stand. When you are ready, decide that *you* will have the last word. Not the diagnosis, the tragedy, the accident, the divorce, the death, the bankruptcy, the addiction, the sentence, or the disability... *you*. Don't rush here. You are going to want to, but you can't. You'll be *ready* when you feel a tiny bit curious about what life might look like on the other side. When that happens, take a stand.

Rebuild with what you've got. Life after a loss is like being shipwrecked at sea and having to build a life raft from the rubble while trying to keep your head above the water. Nothing that worked before is going to work again. Not your faith, not your habits, not your relationships, not your self-talk, not your escape mechanisms... nothing. There is no going back to 'the way things used to be'. You are building something *completely new* using what you have... and what you have is seemingly ruined. However, it's not ruined. The process of rebuilding involves taking stock of who you *really* are. It's what the storm *couldn't* destroy. That, along with your spirit (which is stronger than you know) is more than enough. You'll see.

If you don't believe you can make the shift... I will believe it for you until you can believe it for yourself. I am already praying for you.

Lorraine Tilbury

Dr. Lorraine Tilbury, a multilingual veterinarian, lectures on three continents, from India to Arizona, working with horses so that they can be the Eponaquest© guides and coaches of her seminars.

Her inspired and humorous creations reflect her way of life and the wisdom of her soul. She practices 'Intentional Creativity©,' a powerful approach that Lorraine uses in her teachings, supported by her horses who will 'whisper' their advice to you...she will teach you how to listen to them. Lorraine spent forty-five years understanding that her dreams were within reach - now she can help you fulfill yours!

Learn more about Lorraine:

Website: www.lorrainetilbury.com

Facebook: https://www.facebook.com/horsepowerinternational/

Twitter and Instagram: @ltilbu

Chapter 18

My Personal 'Horse Shift'

By Lorraine Tilbury

You're living my dream! That comment was posted by a work colleague after I shared a photograph of the 16th-century priory that we had just bought as our new home in the heart of the Loire Valley in France. I'm still living in this beautiful place. My life today, however, is very different from what it was when we first purchased it.

I arrived here expecting to continue a relatively tranquil life. However, things did not turn out as expected. A series of events led to a huge shift in my life. While it seemed traumatic at the time, I realize now that it was a crucial step to get to where I am now, and I'm in fact very grateful for it. I'm sharing the story of my shift with the hope that it will inspire others to consider these kinds of similar events – if they occur in their own lives – to be an amazing opportunity to move to something much more rewarding for their lives.

So, what happened? After spending fifteen years in the same company, I was looking for a change. I was stagnating because my family constraints did not fit with the usual career path that required international mobility before progressing to global leadership roles; as a result, I was getting bored professionally; so

I was searching for other professional opportunities. When I did find a job somewhere else, I met great resistance from my husband. My initiative required that he change where he was working, and this was a great source of stress for him.

During our discussions, I realized that after spending eleven years in a region of France that I did not particularly appreciate, moving elsewhere was a matter of survival for me. I was going to move whether he was coming or not – and I told him that. You can imagine how that went over! To my surprise, he accepted the idea, and the entire family packed everything up and came out to join me in the Loire Valley, more than 400 miles from where we had been living.

The transition went relatively smoothly at first. We found our beautiful dream house, our children adjusted to their new schools, and my husband found a very satisfactory business partnership close to home. However, this new, stabilized situation was not to last. Some serious unexpected obstacles in the R&D division arose in my new company, resulting in the shutting down of the very site that I had just joined barely three years previously. Simultaneously, the massive global subprime financial crisis hit, and job availability dried up in the region. I could only find a similar level of pay in Paris, 200 miles away from home. Consequently, I rented a small flat in Paris where I would live on weekdays, only coming home on weekends.

There I was, a wife and mother to three children with a demanding career, suddenly on my own for the entire week, from Monday to Friday - with my own place - in the center of Paris. I absolutely adored being completely on my own all week. I imagine you can see where my story might be going...

I ended up getting involved in an affair and decided to leave my husband. He seemed completely taken by surprise and appeared quite devastated. Imagine my own astonishment, then – when I discovered, barely ten days after our breakup – that he had started dating a neighbor of ours who instantly moved in with him into our house. Even more surprising to me was my own reaction to what he had done. For years, I had dreamed of finding a way to escape my marriage, yet I was devastated by his rocket-speed re-entry into another relationship.

My unexpected strong reaction led to deep introspection about why I was reacting that way. I decided that I didn't want to leave without giving a chance to discuss what was going on, to see if we could find a way to improve our twenty-plus-year relationship together. So (predictably, perhaps, of a 'typical' midlife crisis chronology), I decided to come back to live in our house. That was when things started to get interesting. My job was still 200 miles away in Paris, so I was coming home several times a week. He informed me that he had no intention of coming back to live with me since I'd taken the initiative to leave.

Less than one month later, he had broken up with his mistress and decided to return home. However, this was not the end of his extra-marital relationship, as it became apparent that he was maintaining contact with her. She was claiming to be depressed, perhaps even suicidal.

This went on from April to early November of the same year, when he announced that he had decided he was going to return to live with her after Thanksgiving. I don't think I've ever had a more abysmal Thanksgiving! There I was, letting him stay in the house even though he'd announced his intention to leave... why in the world was I doing this? At the same time, my company had restructured – and I had lost my job – so I was putting forward a professional and experienced persona in job interviews while facing drama and turmoil at home, resulting in tremendous personal strain.

I had understood, through therapy, that my husband was an abusive alcoholic and that my family had grown up in a climate of verbal and emotional abuse of which I was utterly unaware, having myself grown up in a similar environment. It had been a gradual shift 'downhill', so to speak, over the years of marriage, without me realizing what was happening.

My husband's terms of endearment towards me went from 'My little canary', to 'sow', and then 'stinking bitch' – in French (but it sounded just as bad). His insults always came with a slightly amused, mocking attitude, and I was told that I was 'too sensitive' or 'had no sense of humor' when I protested.

Gaslighting was another common practice I was subjected to; my husband would say one thing, then a few days later state the complete opposite conclusion, never acknowledging what he had said previously. He even told me once that 'He knew me better than I knew myself', a characteristic statement that is cited *verbatim* as an example of verbal abuse in Patricia Evans' classic book, *Verbal Abuse*.

A particularly memorable episode of gaslighting revolved around horseback riding lessons (horses had always been an unfulfilled passion of mine), when I signed up for weekly evening lessons after our first child was born. The change in schedule meant that he would have to do some caregiving of our young baby one evening per week, so naturally, I consulted with him about it beforehand. He agreed to it with no fuss or complaint in what appeared to be a normal, cooperative conversation. He'd already done this kind of thing before for my business trips. The following week, during a conversation with him, while I was at work, I reminded him that it was Thursday, the day I'd be coming home late because of my riding lesson, as we'd discussed. He was livid, furious to 'discover' that I was coming home late, accusing me of neglecting the family without informing him, carrying on so much that after the phone call. I hid in the office bathroom to cry my eyes out.

After years of victimization and abuse, I had reached my limit. I was working away from home five days a week. My children were feeling the stress of the abusive family environment. My life looked like something out of a soap opera! I had hesitated for many months to continue with the divorce. Surely life on my own would be better than being married to an alcoholic, subjected to emotional and verbal abuse. I was ready to draw a line in the sand; I called the lawyer to make an appointment to start divorce proceedings and informed my husband. Low and behold, setting that boundary resulted in him ending his relationship with his mistress. I decided to stay with him and try for a fresh start.

I don't remember how I came upon the book that led to the beginning of my personal shift. It's called *The Tao of Equus*, written by Linda Kohanov, and it describes her own transformational experience in contact with horses on her ranch in Arizona. Her experience with horses 'spoke' to me, as it reflected something that I would have liked to experience myself with horses, but at the time did not feel at all capable of doing so.

I looked at instructors teaching her method who were located close to where I was working. This led to my participation in several workshops, including an in-depth personal development intensive seminar called 'The Nature of Wisdom'. Deep introspection and a reflection on what needed to end and what was going to be my new beginnings, accompanied by the silent yet strong support of the horses who accompanied us during this workshop was the big shift for me. I re-discovered the value of my intuition, something that I'd paid much more attention to as a child, but neglected as I entered adulthood. I learned that my intuition communicated with me through body sensations; there is indeed some literal truth to those expressions 'going with my gut' or 'I feel it in my bones'. I discovered how I could extract the information behind those physical sensations to understand what my intuition was communicating to me. My interaction with 'horse-guides' via the Eponaquest approach taught me that it was time to set boundaries, to stand in my own power and to stand up for what I needed for my own self-care so I could thrive in my environment and in my life. I was ready to do whatever it took for me to get there.

Upon my return home from the last week of the series of workshops, our oldest son commented that I looked younger. The realization of what needed to end, where I was and where I wanted to go, had shed years of stress and worry. I was ready to move on, and it was much clearer to me what I would accept and what I would no longer accept. I set a time limit for myself from which I would instigate divorce proceedings if my husband were still drinking. That was when the universe (or a 'coincidence', if you still call these things that) stepped in and brought me the most beautiful gift, and on my birthday too!

My husband, who was in complete denial about his drinking problem, had a serious accident while returning home from a party that took place less than four miles from home, destroying the car and narrowly escaping death, had he not automatically put his seatbelt on. Part of the routine hospital examination in accidents is the level of alcohol in the blood, and his level was one at which only a chronic alcoholic would still be able to function. My husband had no memory of leaving the party, and no memory of the accident after he woke up in the hospital. As soon as he regained consciousness, he was greeted with these words: "Hello sir! You're an alcoholic." The affirmation hit him like a ton of bricks, and finally, he understood that he truly did have a problem. It was the last time he touched a drop of alcohol; he went to rehab, and he has not been drinking for nearly six years now.

This was a wonderful development of course, and I'm still thankful for how it transpired. It was a very important step, but only the first step. Alcoholism exaggerated the abusive behavior that was already there when he was sober. The next step was another huge initiative on my part that I was able to pull off as a result of 'mastering my shift': I asked that he attend abuse therapy for men. He had grown up in a highly dysfunctional family environment, of which he was partially aware. My request was initially met with a flat-out refusal. "What?" he exclaimed, "sit around in a group with men who beat their wives!? Never!"

"Fine," I said. "I'm still hopeful that we will find a solution so that we can stay together. I don't want to get a divorce right now with the children still at home, so I will merely co-inhabit with you until you do what I request of you, or until all our children leave home. Then I will plan to leave too if you still haven't fulfilled my request by then." It took two years - seven hundred and thirty days - until my husband finally came to me one day. "I don't like living like this!" he growled.

"Well," I said, "You know what you need to do to change it!" He ranted and raved at me. "This is just another stupid request, like so many other useless ones you've imposed upon me! Remember the sex therapy sessions you demanded? Boy, those were *really* useless! You're the one who has a problem, not me! I'm not going to sit around with a bunch of wife-beaters!"

I was steadfast in my resolution to stick to my demand. "You don't have to attend a group session" I replied. "You can have an individual session."

"Oh all right then, if that's the only thing that will change how we're living together, then I'll humor your ridiculous, unreasonable request! You'll have to drive me there since I don't have my license back yet."

An appointment was set. The drive there was peppered with grumpy mutterings of "Stupid woman and her hare-brained ideas" and "I don't see why you're forcing me to do this," and the like.

I parked the car, he disappeared into the treatment center, and I waited with bated breath. Forty-five minutes later, he re-emerged and climbed into the car in silence. I started the drive home, not daring to ask even one question about the session, for fear of him seizing the opportunity to cancel any future attendance. Finally, I thought of a neutral enough question. "Did you have to pay anything?" I asked. "Not this time," he replied. I remained utterly neutral and inexpressive on the outside, but on the inside, I was jumping up and down yelling, *Hurray! He's going to go there again!*

To this day, I still don't know exactly how this men's verbal abuse group approaches their clients for the first time; but it was *very* effective and I'm forever thankful. He went there for two years, eventually participating in group therapy. It has dramatically changed the dynamics of our family and greatly improved our interactions even though there is still a *very* long way to go.

Experiential learning with horses connected with me the unseen aspects of life that I'd often read about, but had never fully integrated. I was fascinated by accounts of near-death experiences, and the book *Life after Life* (one of the very first to discuss them, published in the 1970s when I was a child) brought me tremendous hope and excitement. So there is something more to us than our physical life on earth! What an amazing adventure awaits when we die!

I have gradually come to embrace the concept that life really is *exactly* what we expect or need it to be. I learned to ride the wave of 'shift' as it happened, observing, breathing, trusting that my soul or my intuition would know what to focus on next. All I have to do is learn to listen to its guidance, and set in place the actions – however small – that will contribute to singing the song inside me. I have lived what I need to live to be where I am today: an entrepreneur supporting the personal and professional transformation of others through creativity and interaction with my horse herd.

Our experiences are *all* good; they bring to us what we need to fulfill our life purpose, to sing our 'soul song'. Horses helped me connect with my inner self and provided the focus for unearthing my path. Now I want to share that approach with others with the hope that it will help them find their path as well – the HorsePowered Path!

Lysa L. Young

Lysa has over twenty years' experience in truth-telling and faith. In accordance with God's will, Lysa believes life is amazing when she is supporting others to live life with a clear vision.

She has studied self-help and integrated wellness and is a graduate of the American Personal Training Academy. Her mission is to inspire wellness in the plus-sized community.

Lysa has mentored children and teens, on many different platforms, for over thirty years. She presently welcomes and inspires teens from all over the world.

She was born and raised in Cambridge Massachusetts but currently lives in Framingham with her two daughters Sahara and Kolbi.

Learn more about Lysa:

Email: clearvisioncoaching@gmail.com

Instagram: crystal clear vision 2017

Facebook: Lysayoung clear vision coaching and consulting

Chapter 19

Hearing God's Voice

By Lysa L. Young

I had no money and no one to help me. I wanted to give up. That was when I heard the words, *Lysa, I have brought you this far. Hold on*. I knew these were God's words; spoken for me to hear. His message was clear – I am strong, and I had to keep going!

This was the second time in my life I heard a powerful male voice calling my name. However, there were no people around at either time. The first time I did not take strong committed action, as I could not hear the message clearly. Honestly, at the time, it freaked me out. My first inclination was that due to all the tragedies and traumas in my early life I was 'hearing things'. That first time it was simply my name, *Lysa, Lysa*. Only now, with faith and hindsight, can I see that the voice was trying to startle me awake. I needed a strong wake-up call, but because I was standing on shaky ground, I could not feel nor hear the message.

As you can probably guess, my life until this point had not been the stuff from which dreams are made. The messy details that combined to make my life to this point are enough to fill a set of encyclopedias. I have always tried to see the lessons and power in the journey. I rarely mired in the muck or focused on the negative even then, so I won't begin now. For the longest time, I did not have a spiritual belief system to build my life upon.

I can see now that God was always shining a light on my path. One gift I had throughout life – no matter how many curveballs I was attempting to catch – was the ability to be there for others through their pain. While there is some joy and satisfaction in supporting others, the act of being a savior left me empty. The emptiness and pain inside started to show on the outside. At my rock bottom, I had ballooned up to four hundred pounds in weight. I was sad. I stayed inside; sleeping my life away because it was too difficult to walk. The man of my life had disappeared. While I didn't realize it would be a brief reunion, rather than the marriage I hoped for, it did bring my greatest joy – my daughter Sahara.

While I was a positive force for others in their lives, I had never been ready to stand up for my own life. I arrived at yet another valley, a cavern really, when I realized I had spent my last dollar. I could not see a clear path to climb out; I was frozen in a fog. The thought crossed my mind, *This is it, I'm done.*

My breakdown triggered what would become a cornerstone for many breakthroughs I needed the rest of my life. We have now come full circle in my story to the time when I believe God spoke to me the second time. Although I knew there was a lesson to learn, I did not immediately begin trusting that I knew what it was.

What I experienced immediately after that second message was miraculous. I found a $20 bill three times that week. *Three times!* I knew this was God looking out for me. I had courageously conquered so many things in life. I would not, nor could not toss God's faith and belief in me away. I knew I could break through this financial challenge if I gave it half a chance. What I didn't yet realize was that the financial part of the story was not the gem.

I began looking deep inside myself for answers. I realized I was not only in a financial crisis, but I also had no deep spiritual connection to my God. I knew I had the capacity to trust him. That was the first step. When I began trusting that he had a plan in mind for me, it was like an awakening. It was if I were seeing the world for the first time. I noticed the beauty in nature and the people around me.

Next, I immersed myself in the process of building my faith. I wanted to uncover a deep spiritual bond with him. I also wanted to discover what God's greater plan for me was! With my energy focused, I knew it was my turn. Step by step, my process of becoming my own savior began. My trust in him led me to trust others. However, my *true* journey began when I started trusting myself. Only then could an understanding of using trust as a guidance system emerge.

I began to see my value and believe in myself with a steadfastness I had only known for others. As my faith grew, I felt lighter. I expanded with each page I read in the books I had gathered or been gifted. I opened myself up to others – moving cautiously. I attracted (with God's help) trustworthy women into my life. Although I considered them friends, they did not coddle me. They did not just tell me they understood my pain and allow me to cry on their shoulders. Although it was not my nature, they would never stand for me being a victim or martyr in the challenges that came up. These women held me to the dreams and plans I made for my life. As each one brought her wisdom for her time in my life, I saw them as angels sent from God. I began seeing the beauty in my own heart as my faith expanded. Having this series of women by my side, I grew stronger. As I focused on the joy and beauty around me, in the trees, sky, and flowers – my world opened again. Relationships and opportunities arrived as I radiated the joy within through my smiles.

The trials and tribulations had caused me to close off from the world. Now I consider those times as blessings that created the insight who to let into my life. I have learned to choose my friends and supporters wisely. My wisdom is based on my newfound beliefs and trust in my higher power, my God.

My journey continues today. I follow the same path when faced with decisions or dilemmas. I look inward first and listen to God; he guides me and sends the right people into my life. I now choose to accept what is offered in times of need. I ask him to help me find the true path.

I believe we all have the answers inside of us. We just need to listen. God comes to us when we are connected to him through silence. Whether you believe in God, another deity, the universe, or your own higher voice within – plan periods of silence. Try it. You'll be amazed at the messages that present themselves to you. No matter what you name the source of the inner voice inside – trust that they speak to you for your greater good. Believe the messages. Hand the messy details over to the guidance system that resides inside you. Trust that it's not your job. Your job is to open your heart, ask for help, trust that the answers will come, and then act on the answers provided.

Today I walk tall with courage, trust, and confidence that God has my back. I am proud to be in partnership with him! My life has molded me into the courageous and honest woman that I am today. I live in joy and passion – raising my daughter to be a strong woman on her own spiritual journey. The other children I have been given the privilege and honor to raise are strong adults. I smile each day with the knowledge that I have built a solid foundation for all our lives.

Ratika Hansen

Ratika Hansen is a mommy to twin boys, a wife, and a marketing manager in the high-tech industry. She is also a long-standing student of personal growth, devoting the last fifteen years to learning from a variety of masters. Her life purpose is to shine her light in the world in the form of acceptance, laughter, inspiration, and love.

As a best-selling author, a certified Passion Test facilitator and credentialed Make A Difference seminar leader, she has shared her personal life shifts to inspire thousands of people to lead passionate lives. Ratika helps them to bring their light to their relationships, their careers, and their communities.

Learn more about Ratika:

Websites: www.ToYourPassionateLife.com

http://inspiredbythepassiontest.com/

Facebook: www.Facebook.com/ToYourPassionateLife

Chapter 20

Madness, Sadness, and a Little Badassness

By Ratika Hansen

My shift downward happened gradually...one sweet, subtle celebration at a time. As an intensely committed student of personal growth, with a caring village of wise people guiding me, I thought I had prepared myself well for each one. Yet I found myself ever so lost, disenchanted with life, and unrecognizable to myself after five whirlwind years of big life changes.

From what I had observed and heard growing up, these were the changes that everyone looked forward to. These were the changes that were *supposed* to happen – the major milestones that indicated my success as an adult. However, each one left me emptier – not more fulfilled – as the world had promised me. In hindsight, I see why, and of course, it has everything to do with me. I share my story with the hope that if you are blessed with these same wonderful life events, you are better equipped to enjoy them for the magic that they really are. Let my madness and sadness guide you on your own path to badassness!

Once upon a time, I was on top of my game. I was enjoying being single in a new city that I had quickly made my own. I was a powerful leader in all aspects of my life, excelling professionally, and clearly understanding my value at work. I appreciated and was appreciated by my customers and co-workers. I laughed and pondered and explored a lot with a sweet circle of amazing, inspiring, fun-loving friends. I was giving greatly to causes that mattered to me and made a difference for others. I had bought my first home and thoughtfully painted every wall in the place to match the different facets of my personality. I glowed with an aura that brightened my world.

That aura caught one man's eye, and after some conscious deliberating, I found myself in a serious, long-distance relationship with him.

A year later, I had the opportunity to start a new job – one I had wanted for several years. To my instant and impulsive delight, that job could also relocate me closer to my beau. I knew that I did not want to be the girl who moved across the country for a *guy*, only to feel stranded if we broke up. Instead, I wanted to move across the country for the *job*, and love that the guy happened to be there too. Fully immersed in my transformational work, I was clear about who I was and who I wanted to be. Contemplating the pitfalls that my decision could bring on, I examined each path and created the way I wanted it to go. With the support of my loving network, I did the work to make it so. That was a shift that I did right. And thank goodness – because when that relationship did end, as devastated as I was, I could not blame him or myself for my sudden pangs of loneliness in a city that I had moved to *for him*... because I was already very clear that I did not move there for him at all.

While I did not fall victim to my loneliness, I was still, in fact, very lonely. I did not have a solid foundation for myself in this new city. This wasn't *my* city – it was 'our' city from the minute I landed here. When we broke up, I felt very lost. It was as if the rug had been ripped out from under me and I was falling, falling, falling. There was very little here that reflected who I was. In the moment that I needed it most, the light I needed to remind me of my essence had been replaced with darkness.

Utterly heartbroken, I began the process of starting over to make this city mine. I attracted a man who introduced me to the wonders of a relationship that I had not experienced before. Again, I deliberated very consciously before allowing our relationship to deepen. At least I had figured out that part of life shifts! Hypersensitive to what had been missing in my last relationship, this man healed those parts of me and filled those voids beyond my dreams. It was, in many ways, the fairytale princess fantasy that I had wanted for my life since I was a little girl.

After dating for a year, we got engaged, and I began my preparation for the big life change called marriage. When I walked down the aisle, I thought I was ready. I was inspired by my own progress and sure that one day, I would be on stage with my husband, in front of other committed students of personal growth. I wanted to be the one guiding them in how to have magical marriages of their own.

For the first several years of our marriage, it was my mission to make this union heaven on earth. All of my efforts were focused on this – every vision I wrote, every goal I created, and every action plan I set in motion had this end result at its core. I quickly realized that marriage is much harder than I thought. It uncovered and exposed sides of my personality that I had either hidden away or not developed at all.

My marriage required strength in areas that I was weak. I found that I was not good at voicing my opinion if it was different from his. I stifled my feelings when they were negative. I was challenged to consider and respect opinions that were not aligned with mine – something that I was not used to doing. As a single person, if I really disagreed with someone, I simply distanced myself from him or her. I couldn't do that in my marriage. I didn't *want* to do that in my marriage. I learned, much to my dismay, that I still had a lot to learn to be successful in my marriage.

Gathering up all of my self-empowerment tools, I set out to 'fix' my marriage – ever so determined to crack the code, rewrite my destiny, and restart my perfect married life. I knew I could do it. I had written and achieved so many of my goals. I had always created the life I wanted, the life I had envisioned for myself, the life I knew I deserved. After many failed attempts, I felt sad and alone. I tried harder month after month to find the bliss of the 'honeymoon phase', and yet, it eluded me. At the end of my rope, I wasn't sure how to bring on the growth required to have the happy marriage I had dreamed of – and that was a very scary feeling.

In making my life exclusively about my singular pursuit of a great marriage, I had lost myself. I lost the things that mattered most to me, that defined me, that filled my heart and nourished my soul. Yet, despite my daily struggles, I still had no idea that such a massive shift downward was even happening.

Two years and two months into our marriage, we welcomed two baby boys into our family.

Boom. I thought marriage was teaching me what I was made of. I had no idea what being a mother was going to reveal. This was another one of those 'being as ready as you can be – and yet being nowhere close' kind of everyday changes that nearly every new mother goes through. Now I had not one but three hearts, minds, and schedules to be mindful of, besides my own, which was already being sorely neglected.

In my first five years of motherhood, I took on another lofty goal. Any time I wasn't spending trying to make my marriage work, I was now focusing on being the best mom I could be. I read the books, listened to the podcasts, and watched the webinars. I put a lot of pressure on myself to establish the perfect parenting philosophy, rules and routines, and touching traditions early on.

I knew that it wasn't a matter of *if* I was going to screw up my kids, but rather how well I could equip them to deal with *how* I screwed them up. Even so, I still held fast to rigid and sometimes conflicting ways of being with them — not equipping them properly at all. With a laundry list of things I wanted to teach them, I was disappointed in my inability to be the 'perfect' mom and constantly worried that I was not raising them 'right'. This took a toll on my self-confidence and left me feeling helpless in caring for my babies. I was sad, frustrated, and overwhelmed, so far removed from the brightly shining aura I once knew myself to be.

I had not realized that each moment with my boys is a teachable moment for them – and for me. They often uncover unhealed wounds that I used to accept as my personality, dare I say, even my divinity. My boys have 'pushed buttons' that have exposed a lifetime of abuse to my soul. In getting to the root of and healing these buttons, I am growing ever closer to my true self, my authentic self, the essence of my divinity. I am beginning to shine my light again.

It took me five years to catch my breath and get my head above water after all of these changes. Once I did, I could see how deeply severed I had become from my soul. I invoked an immediate facelift on my life. This shift was a downward-on-the-way-upward kind of shift. I took a long hard look at turning my life on its head, redefining it from the ground up. Over the past several years, these shifts had slowly brought me to a point of dull pain, speckled with moments of sweetness. It was time to consciously change the trajectory of my life!

I started by returning to the basics, to the steps I purposefully took on a regular basis to create the life I used to love. First, I created an annual goal for myself – a goal to get myself back on track. Then I created a plan with a monthly checklist of activities that would help me achieve my goal. Finally, I began to schedule those things each month, and I did not give them up. I protected and prioritized these activities to ensure my return to my best self.

I also returned to a path of conscious living. I enrolled in a conscious parenting class, a mindful living course, and took on a daily yoga and meditation practice. These have re-introduced me to the glowing woman I used to be before I had to schedule time to connect with myself. With a much fuller life now, I know that doing so is vital to me being and bringing my best to my world.

We each have unique gifts to bring to the world. If our hearts, minds, and souls are compromised, we cannot access, let alone share these gifts. Here are some lessons from my journey. In the face of life's inevitable shifts, I hope they will help you stay profoundly connected to your gifts.

Lesson 1: know yourself profoundly. Take the time to observe your thoughts and test your assumptions. Explore your passions, define your core values, and create your life vision. See what makes your heart sing and dance with joy. Watch what scares you, threatens you, and saddens you. Do the work to uncover the source of these and heal them. Understand yourself inside and out. This is where your peace and happiness begins and ends; within you.

Lesson 2: expand from your heart to create your life so that you glow ever so brightly in it. It is from this place only that you will sparkle for yourself and your world. This includes being firmly planted where you are. Establish a meaningful relationship with your routine and your surroundings, in your home, your work, and your community. All of this will serve as a mirror to remind you of who you are when you have forgotten – which often happens in the midst of shifts. It is a bit of identity insurance, if you will, as life brings dizzying changes, to establish something solid and stable upon which you can lean. Create a strong foundation for yourself made of those things that make you who you are.

Lesson 3: deliberate deeply and widely about your choices. Consider all possibilities and how you feel about each one. Then choose your path and go for it with all of your heart, knowing you did your homework. Trust implicitly that you made the best decision you could for yourself in the moment. In doing so, you will avoid blaming yourself or anyone else should that choice later take you down a 'dark' path. Away from the suffering of that self-torture, you will rapidly and gracefully move into creativity and action to chart a new course for yourself anytime the need arises.

Lesson 4: look for the lesson and the opportunity in every upset. There is always a place to grow and evolve in the face of disappointment. What reality are you resisting? What expectation do you have that was not met? What can you let go of? Where do you need a boundary? Where can you speak your truth? Is there a deeper source of your upset that this incident has invoked? The best way to heal an upset is to learn and grow through it. You will emerge lighter, brighter, and more evolved on the other side.

Lesson 5: prepare as much as you would like for the shifts in your life. Then be open to the elements of your shift that you were not expecting. Recognize that you will never be 100% prepared for everything life sends your way, and that is ok. Go with the flow when life surprises you. If you stay connected to who you are, you will always have everything you need inside you to navigate the surprises that come with your shifts.

Lesson 6: the breath is where it's at. Adopt a mindfulness practice, including meditation, yoga, and regular spiritual lessons to most quickly return to your divinity. While it is the last lesson, it has had the biggest impact on my journey of big life shifts.

Do not be afraid of life's big changes (or small ones, for that matter). Shifts are good, whether they happen with your conscious consent or not. I know that had my path thus far been different, I would not have had the opportunities to grow through my dark moments into a new, brighter, more evolved version of myself. I don't regret my choices – even the ones that took me 'downward' in my path. It's all relative. It is only from the darkness below, from the madness and sadness, that one can shine brightly at new heights of badassness!

May you shine too!

Robyn McTague

Robyn McTague is a master holistic healer who helps adults and children increase their vibration so they can create a life of choice and freedom.

Robyn has trained in a multitude of disciplines from psychology, business, energy and healing systems and conflict resolution.

She has experienced both breast cancer and hepatitis C – amongst other challenges in her life – and has been able to heal and move forward.

Her mission is to assist others in their healing journeys, in a safe, practical, and gentle way.

Her vision is to create a world of kindness – one person at a time.

Learn more about Robyn:

Website: http://robynmctague.com/

FB: https://www.facebook.com/MasterHolisticHealer/

Linked In:
https://www.linkedin.com/in/robyn-mctague-b6410610/

Chapter 21

From Sofa to Soaring

By Robyn McTague

For the majority of my life, I was concerned about being perfect and meeting the expectations of others. I needed to prove myself and took on more than my share of responsibility. I learned from a mother, who was unable to be a parent due to her own mental illness. I juggled a full-time job, plus doing union work and strata council work. There wasn't time for me anywhere in this equation. It was all about doing for others and taking up the slack because that's what I believed I needed to do to be loved.

Then my world came crashing down in the year 2000. At the age of forty-four, I was diagnosed with early-stage breast cancer. I was considered young to be diagnosed.

I was in shock. As were my friends and family. I was the healthy one. I ate well, exercised, was a non-smoker, and my weight was normal. I felt like a zombie. I was walking around, going through the motions; I was numb and had checked out.

Decisions were made quickly. The options were to take off the breast or remove tissue and do radiation. I didn't feel like it was much of a choice, so I went with option two. I kept going without really questioning anything; there didn't seem time for that.

I did what I could with the limited Internet that was available then. Cancer was now my job, and I used the local cancer agency for help and information.

Surgery was booked within two weeks. The post-surgery appointment came with more bad news; there were no clear margins (this means the cancer was not entirely removed). A friend of a friend had warned me about this, and here it was. I was still getting over the first surgery, and now I was being told I needed more. The cancer that remained needed to be cut out – and soon. My surgeon was heading out of town, so again we booked surgery for two weeks' time.

At my next appointment, I was given the report to take home. I was frantic when I read it. I felt defeated, no clear margins again! I rang the clinic in a panic, only to find out I was given the wrong report. Phew!

More stress and worry, issues of trust? You bet. See what happens?

From there I went to the oncology clinic to have my body 'mapped' for radiation. I felt like a slab of meat. I was measured and two tiny blue dots (permanent tattoos), were added to my body. This was to mark where the radiation would go.

Radiation treatment was like going to work. I had to psyche myself up – Monday to Friday – sixteen treatments. I was in countdown mode. I was driven to the cancer agency, and I would undress, wait, line up on the bed, get zapped, change and drive home. Each time left me feeling worse. More exhaustion, fatigue, burning hot skin, and a beautiful new red square on my chest.

Food was hard to think about; I had no energy, no appetite, and no real taste for anything. Sitting on the sofa wasn't even an option. I was forced to listen to what my body needed. The message was, *Lie down*. Sitting wasn't restful enough. Stress was high, my body felt tight and restricted. I was thankful for the relaxation groups at the clinic and my local hospital up the street.

Friends would ask what I wanted or needed. I really didn't know. I read an article in a magazine and used lines from it to get me off the hook. "Don't ask me what I want to do tomorrow; all I can figure out is what I want to do next. I can't even think of what I want for lunch." I was living in the moment, though not in a good way. I ended up spending a lot of time on my sofa. Alone, no noise, no sound, no TV – just my thoughts and me.

I began to connect the dots. Six months before the diagnosis, I kept hearing this voice in my head. *Something big is going to happen in your life.* I was curious, and when some event would happen I would hear the message, *No, not big enough.* That was until the diagnosis and the realization this was the big moment. The question was, what next?

The week prior to the diagnosis, I had been attending a workshop on the beautiful Cortes Island at Hollyhock, a non-profit educational institute that advances consciousness. I experienced holotropic breathwork for the first time. During this intense breath work, I released so much dark emotion. Parts of myself I had kept hidden, pushed deep down. The abuse, the anger, parts of me that were not lovable. I felt the joy of release as I connected to my spirit self.

I began the process of feeling into my entire body, every molecule, every part of the RNA and the DNA. In movement, I felt pain release; I really felt my body for the first time, in its fullness. I was tapping into a part of me that had long been forgotten. I felt a physical transformation and became a turtle. This began a new relationship with my body.

When I walked into the cancer agency, what was in the foyer? An art project with pictures of turtles. Synchronicity? There was also display of words: strength, stability, longevity, wisdom. Messages I needed to hear. Years later I visited the Galapagos and met Lonesome George, a giant tortoise believed to be over one hundred and fifty years of age. I felt the wisdom, strength, and patience he emanated.

To help with my recovery, I met with a music therapist, and we created a meditation cassette with sounds that I love. I lay on the table and felt a beautiful green light come through the window, infusing my body with healing energy. I was finally listening to my spirit and knew everything would be ok.

I continued living life on my sofa for several months. I was finally not afraid to go inside myself and find out what was truly going on in there. I knew I couldn't avoid my life anymore. You've heard of people's lives flashing before their eyes before they die? For me, it was a long slow revisit to the pain in my life. You may remember the show 'This is Your Life'. That's what it felt like.

I revisited past traumas of myself and those I loved: teen suicides, my mother's suicide attempts, sexual, physical and emotional abuse. When I couldn't cry for myself, I would cry for others. I needed the release; I had to let it all out. Holding that emotion in for so long helped to create the situation I was in. I finally saw how emotionally shut down I was. I believe that when we do not listen to our spirit, the last place we will listen is when our physicality is involved; I am a slow learner.

Time carried on, and I attended the breast cancer support group. The doctors suggested a drug called Tamoxifen. It was scary; the drug to stop the reoccurrence of breast cancer could cause other cancers. I needed help; the women I talked with were all post-menopausal, so I was left to decide on my own. Once more, I went along to get along. The side effects were full menopausal symptoms: weight gain, crying for no reason, high emotion, and night sweats. I would need to go through the menopausal symptoms again when my body said it was time.

My symptoms improved slightly, and after two years I said I had enough, I would not take the medication for five years. I refused to live in fear anymore. I knew within my body that I had learned the lesson I needed to learn and cancer was a thing of the past.

During a visit to the cancer agency, I saw information about the Callanish Society. I had taken a brochure and set it aside. I had completed treatment and wasn't sure what was next. I needed to discover my new 'normal'. One of the women in my relaxation group had attended and encouraged me to apply for the retreat. Shortly after, I received a call and was asked if I wanted to go. There had been a cancellation, and I had an hour to decide if I wanted to leave the next day. I knew it was right, I could feel it in my body. I got a cat sitter and started packing.

Quadra Island was a magical place, even in February. I had not felt so loved, nurtured and cared for in a very long time. There were eight women in our group. We connected with laughter, tears, joy, and release. We talked and listened deeply – from our souls. We talked about death, dying, living, and everything in between. Several of the women were very ill and in last stages of life. It was an honor to be part of their journey. We sat in the hot tub and expressed our doubts, joys, and sorrows.

Looking at other women across the tub, I was surprised when I would see whole breasts. Breast cancer had consumed me, and I was able to shake myself out of that. We had movement, nature, music, camaraderie and the ability to just be ourselves – cancer and all. There were no judgments, no hiding how we were feeling to spare our friends and loved one's feelings.

During a session with a counselor, one discussion clarified what role cancer played in my life. It was not about loss, I'd had plenty of loss in my life. It was about my spiritual growth. I knew I would never be the same. I felt like something had broken open within me. I could breathe again, acknowledge who and where I was, what a relief.

I returned, renewed and connected to myself. I was honored to speak at a fundraiser shortly after to help let others know what a truly healing place it had been. I eventually traveled to see the actual Callanish Stones in Scotland.

Eventually, my doctor was pushing me to get back to work, and I felt resentful. I had been doing all this healing work, and the old theme came up for me again: where is the time for me? I had been working hard at this cancer game.

My then-boyfriend took me on a trip to Hawaii. Despite having to stay covered up and out of direct sun, I felt relaxed and enjoyed the warm, healing air.

When we got back home, I still felt anxious about returning to work. I went to a counselor and expressed my feelings of vulnerability and emotional weakness. I was unwinding and becoming friends with new emotions.

On the day of my last appointment, there was an earthquake in nearby Seattle.

As I sat in the bathtub, the aftershocks swayed the water and shook the entire building. What a fitting experience for what was to come next.

During the appointment we worked on some energy I felt was stuck in my lower stomach (the second chakra area). It felt like an old survival feeling. She suggested I just continue to sit with it and allow it to come up as it needed to.

Home on the sofa, I surrendered to the information. I felt the world spin as I felt the knowing that I was gay. I felt relieved and afraid at the same time. I knew why I had always felt different and never fitted in. Now my world made sense. I was still afraid to say anything to anyone; I kept it in. I couldn't explain to my doctor why I didn't feel ready to go back to work.

So instead, I focused on another goal. Before cancer, every day at lunchtime, I would workout at the gym. I wanted to be able to return to my workouts and change my clothes without feeling I had to hide my body. A simple sports top was enough to reveal that I no longer had matching breasts. I was lopsided and had one nipple pointing to the ground. It took time, but I reached that goal.

I eventually returned to work. However, I couldn't remember how to do my job. I was devastated and didn't know how I could be around all these stressed out people. I was given project work, and gradually, over another six months, I returned to my former position.

Soon after, I was at a social event and a woman told me about a course that provided energetic shielding and grounding, allowing love in and keeping the negativity out.

This was another of those, 'Yes that's for me' moments. I attended class the following Tuesday.

After the first week, I felt better, what a relief. I could be around people again.

I returned to my union work and was approached to run for president. Without thinking, I said, "No, I'm going to be a healer."

Within a short time of taking the course, I manifested a new job, helping to create a new department that would use many of my skills. Life still had ups and downs. I dealt with lymphedema and wore a sleeve on my arm for a year and a half. I went through several reconstructive surgeries after the initial one failed, including surgery to remove scar tissue.

I continued with my personal healing work, and I also helped others with their journeys by becoming a holistic healer. My vision is to create a world of kindness, one person at a time. One of the biggest lessons has been self-first, and I now teach this amazing course to both adults and children. My goal is to help others heal before they plummet downwards as I did. It is not necessary. What I have learned is that after trauma, whether it is cancer or anything else, we need to find our new 'normal'. Life will not be the same. It's about taking where we are now, accepting and acknowledging our journey. We then need to build on that knowledge, strength, and resiliency to be ourselves in the world.

Here are some insights and suggestions for you:

Self-care is part of self-first. To start, find something that nurtures you. It could be massage, reading, or anything else. If you've forgotten what nurtures you, then don't be afraid to experiment.

Being vulnerable is your strength. Get help when you need it; talk to someone. We can become caught up in our own story and need someone who can see us outside of the frame. Know that is not always family. Peer support is one of many ways you can talk to someone who has been there.

Meditation works. This has been proven scientifically. Find a system that works for you. I have done TM and other methods before I found the TIPA system that works for me. If one doesn't fit, check out another system.

Learn to trust your inner knowingness, which comes from the inside work. Our society has us looking to the external for our answers. They are found within us when we connect to our spirit. Fear is an old story, and you deserve to have the freedom of choice.

Be physical. We often live outside our body. To connect back to ourselves we need to be physical. Walk, do yoga, breathe, and dance. Find the joy in movement. Be gentle and start slowly.

Celebrate every time you do any of the above and build new neural pathways of gratitude.

Samuel Nazer Walsh

Samuel Nazer Walsh is a transformational thought leader in the 'new consciousness movement'. Having traveled the globe extensively for workshops and training under some of the greatest masters of our time, he has discovered the missing pieces to a more fulfilling, enriching and meaningful life. Through his community of heart-centered entrepreneurs who understand socially conscious living, he shares his wisdom on how to lead a life by design as opposed to leading a life by accident. He continues to develop his blueprint for optimal living – living a life of purpose and on purpose.

Learn more about Samuel:

Website: https://www.karmapreneurs.com

Facebook: https://www.facebook.com/samuelnazerwalsh

Twitter: https://twitter.com/SamuelNWalsh

Chapter 22

My Lifelong Friends

By Samuel Nazer Walsh

What does constant struggle look like? Does it ever end? What does betrayal look like? How much is enough? What happens when people go beyond being greedy? Does fear control our lives more than love? Is humanity so heartless and gutless? Is the collective consciousness of the universe so cruel?

January 25th, 1993, a day that I will never forget for the rest of my life. That night, at 10:00 pm precisely, my life changed forever. My best friend, my father, had just passed away. I never realized the impact he had on my life until his physical presence was no longer there, and his body had become lifeless. The death of such a close loved one was different for me this time, as I felt a 'big part' of me had died with him.

Being the first-born child of the family, I received plenty of 'attention' and 'unconditional love' from my parents and grandparents. With my grandparents passing away, my father had filled the void of 'unconditional love' in my life, as he was well aware of how close I was to them. The mourning period had begun moments after his death, and I had no idea what was to follow in my life and what experiences I would have to endure.

When I reflect back at this moment to twenty-four years ago, it is hard to imagine how I managed to survive all these years despite the turbulence. What blessings I must have received to get me through those times; it was a lifetime's worth of lessons.

The mourning period for our family, as is customary within our community and religious traditions, was forty days of solemnness, reflection, prayer, abstinence, tolerance, respect, and humbleness. This was an intense time in my life with emotions running very high; it felt like I was going through roller coaster rides. These emotions became intense with the days that passed; it was a busy time with all the family, friends, and visitors coming from around the world to pay their last respects to my father at his funeral. Many of these visitors stayed on for several weeks to be with the family and support us in our time of deep bereavement. My father was a recognized global leader in our community because of his life's charitable work. He was in a position of high authority due to his influence, connections, and affluence. My father had amassed a lot of wealth through his business ventures at a young age. Upon his death at the tender age of fifty, his legacy was passed on to my brother and I.

His last will and testament was opened thirty days after his death. However, I was privy to the contents of his will three months before his death and was well-informed of all his business affairs, dealings and connections. I was six months shy of my twenty-fifth birthday when my father passed away and to have been burdened with such a big responsibility in looking after his legacy and estate was a daunting task. I was still attending university to complete my business degree.

In the days to come after my father's will had opened, I did not expect that there would be so much turmoil within our extended family. Many family members wanted a piece of our inherited wealth. My father was an intelligent, witty, street-savvy and a wise businessman. He earned his wealth through the hard work and the calculated and profitable business ventures that he executed in his life. Yet extended family members felt he needed to distribute that wealth to them to manage, as my brother and I were still too young and 'raw' to cope with such a big responsibility.

My father, in the year previous to his death, had foreseen what could happen if he passed away as he had a heart transplant done on January 21st, 1992, due to a massive heart attack and bypass surgery was not an option for him. As much as the doctors had reassured him that he would remain well, my father using his intuition, believed that the gift of life that he received from the heart transplant surgery was 'borrowed time'. He felt that his time on this planet was going to be short.

In the year previous to his death, I recall him telling me that he felt that he had completed his life's work and there was only one more important thing that he needed to accomplish. He had decided that he would like to gift some of his wealth to his extended family. My father asked my brother and I in a special meeting with legal counsel in March 1992, if we took issue with him parting with a good portion of his wealth to distribute to his extended family. Both my brother and I were supportive of his wisdom and his act of goodwill because we knew how much his family meant to him. He always said that 'charity starts at home', it was a 'blessing' and a noble deed to him. As my father distributed his wealth to the extended family members in July 1992, it was interesting to observe how they all clustered around, showing us all an enormous amount of love, affection, compassion, and support. I am sure that they were not expecting such generous gifts of cash, and business assets, from my father, and were beyond grateful at the time for his kindness.

The days after the opening of the will became very dark for my brother and I. We were still mourning our father's death. We felt like bandits were surrounding us as we received correspondence from legal counsel representing the different family members who wanted access to our inherited wealth. Legal proceedings commenced within sixty days after the will opening. My brother and I were not open to negotiation or a settlement on my father's estate for additional distributions to the extended family members. We chose to fight as long as we could and risk it all if we needed to. The winner would take it all.

This was not about arrogance and ego for us; it was about fighting for our rights and not allowing family members to take control of something that was not theirs to start with. They had already been given large sums from my father six months prior to his death, and yet they were shameless seeking out more distributions.

With legal proceedings commenced, almost all of our inherited assets were frozen. I started questioning why I was shown an abundant and peaceful life before my father's death, and after his death, suddenly, I was being shown a life of betrayal, greed, and fear. What had changed in the equation of life? Was it the changing of the 'guard'? Was my father just a 'trustee' for the wealth and grace that he had received in his life that was not to be passed on?

With my father's passing, we inherited many so-called 'new friends'. Many people wanted to be in our company. Many came with business proposals, and many wanted to hang out and party with us because we led a life of luxury and had an abundance of material things (shiny objects that are the envy of so many).

The estate litigation dragged on for just over three years after my father's death, and it was ugly. We had accountants, tax accountants, lawyers, tax lawyers, and tax authorities all feasting on estate funds. The cash bleed was very heavy because every family member wanted a share of the estate, so my brother and I had to obtain proper legal representation. The judgment came out in our favor and extended family at that point threatened to continue to escalate matters to the Supreme Court for another trial, which would mean further litigation. I had told my brother that after three years of an intense legal battle, I wanted to resolve matters with our extended family and part ways. I was fed up with the drama, and I was not prepared emotionally or mentally to continue with another litigation.

We came to an arrangement with extended family members after months of deliberations with all the lawyers involved, liquidated all the estate assets and realized that just over 70% of our inheritance was going to be eroded. On hindsight, we would have been better off coming up with a settlement arrangement with our extended family after my father's death when the will had opened, and demands were made upon us for additional distributions.

Inheriting such a big responsibility at such a young age meant I was vulnerable. I had my fair share of constant struggle, and I saw the true nature of people; how they change their attitude towards you, because of their perception of your wealth and affluence. It has had to be one of the greatest lessons I have learned in my life. My father was an extremely wise man and had told me when you throw the weight of money around, people will dance to your tune and perform incredible drama! I did not understand this wisdom when he shared this with me. However, I can truly say that after experiencing what I have – he was spot on.

Life's challenges only make us stronger, and it is up to us individually to search for the lessons. An old adage states that 'success leaves clues'. I believe that 'struggle also leaves clues'. The lengthy period of struggle that I experienced broke me completely. I had reached an abyss in my life and wanted to put an end to the pain and suffering. I did not sign up for all the storms. I felt like old homegrown values of respect, ethics, morals, compassion, courtesy, kindness, and friendship were no longer honored. What I experienced confirms the saying that 'money talks and bullshit walks', also known as 'show me the money'. I kept questioning myself if life had to be led on this path? Was there another way of living and celebrating life?

I had my life channeled. I was told that letting go of my attachment to material possessions and surrendering to the will of the universe was my only option to embrace and accept – especially after so many years of struggling. Failing to do so meant everything that is material in nature and what I knew as 'me', that which is 'attached to me', would be stripped away from me. So what would be the point of prolonging the struggle by living chaotically with hustle and hassle?

As I let go of my attachments, I started finding time and space for contemplation and reflection, which created an environment for peace and harmony in my life. I was learning to live again and was beginning to feel reborn. I began to realize, that in life, 'no one completes you, you complete yourself'. I realized that everything that happened in my life had happened for a reason – to make me a better person. I became wiser, happier, and at peace with myself because I chose to live simply.

My dearest and closest friend told me that I had traded in my 'millions' to get a 'billion'. I smiled at her observation and agreed with her that for what it was worth, I would make that trade an' day. My vault is worth far more to me now than what I had received from my father's estate. What I lost in the process was all worth it for the lessons learned, and experiences gained. As I reflect back on many of the life lessons, I realized that I had rebuilt my life the way I wanted, on my terms, because I trust myself and am unattached to the outcome of my choices. What got me through all of this turbulence is having a gratitude consciousness, the daily practice of gratitude, and taking a gratitude inventory.

The best education we will get from life is not at a formal academic institution, the university of life will teach us what we need to learn. We are students observing, researching, interacting with others, and finding time to play in life's big playgrounds.

Evaluating what life is really about (why are we on this planet at this time, what did we come to achieve, what legacy do we wish to leave behind) empowers us to think differently. If we are 'spiritual beings' having a human experience then how can we make our lives better? How can we lead a more meaningful and fulfilled life?

I will leave you with some points for reflection and consideration.

What can we do to create a better life blueprint?

1. Adopt a practice of finding time and space to reflect and contemplate life and the things that are going on in our chaotic world. How can we make this less chaotic?

2. Adopt a practice of setting intentions of higher frequency. These are not 'goals'. You can gauge an intention when you personally set them as you truly know what you are projecting and asking for.

3. Adopt a practice of finding gratitude in your life and what you are thankful for.

4. Adopt a practice of spreading kindness, cheer, generosity and love - the unconditional kind.

5. Incorporate more humility and humbleness in your life. Catch your spoken and written words so that they don't harm others.

6. Forgive others who you perceive have hurt you and forgive yourself for any shortcomings.

7. Send good energy, love, light and a prayer for those people in regions of the world that are going through turmoil.

8. Life is short, take care of your health. We are given one body. Keep your mind and body nourished.

9. Make an effort for your own personal and spiritual growth. We are entering a turning point in human evolution, the 'great human awakening'.

10. Work towards opening yourself from living from your soul as opposed to living from your mind. This shift on its own will completely transform you as a person.

I have led an eventful and colorful life so far, experiencing my lifelong friends: lifelong mourning, lifelong yearning, and lifelong learning.

Lifelong mourning because of the passing away of loved ones, whose physical presence and wisdom I miss dearly. My grandparents taught me faith and friendship. My father taught me unconditional love and how to become street-savvy.

Lifelong yearning because I miss having the company of unconditional love and true friendship.

Lifelong learning because I have committed to my personal and spiritual growth. I have an unquenchable thirst because when you are not growing, you are dying.

"Gratitude is like a lollipop, it gets sweeter the more you lick it, and if it breaks apart and falls, it still spreads sweetness everywhere the pieces land."

– Samuel Nazer Walsh

Sheila Partridge

Sheila Partridge has lived and traveled all over the world and enjoys connecting with people from many different cultures and backgrounds. She worked in corporate treasury for over fifteen years with major international corporations in London and San Francisco.

Sheila works intensely on her personal development. She attained the highest level of training in VortexHealing® Divine Energy Healing and is a qualified practitioner. She is also a yoga teacher. Her sense of well-being comes from good food, friendships, exercise, relaxation, spiritual oneness, humor and enjoying life.

As a holistic life coach, she helps individuals who are ready to transform their lives.

Learn more about Sheila:

Website: www.sheilapartridge.life

Facebook: https://www.facebook.com/sheila.partridge.359

Email: writeme@sheilapartridge.life

Chapter 23

Freedom After Heartache

By Sheila Partridge

Early one August morning, I remember waking up very early at my friend's apartment in London. I had such an uneasy feeling in my stomach that I knew something was wrong.

We gathered our equipment and went out to Putney Common to practice our yoga. There is nothing quite like being outside at dawn for yoga practice. The air is fresh, with little or no noise from the road traffic; it's heaven.

We practiced our yoga, beginning first with pranayama (the breathing exercises) and then onto the asanas (postures). It was such a treat to practice with a close friend.

After our practice, I still had an unsettling feeling within me. I was overcome with a sense of dread and impending doom. My friend walked me home; when we got back, I checked my phone and found a text message from my then-boyfriend and partner of ten years. I can't remember the exact words, but it amounted to a breakup.

He was living in Dubai at the time, so I tried to call him. I remember stammering and stuttering, as I was unable to speak. My friend heard me crying and came in; I just handed her the phone. She knew something was wrong. I don't recall what my ex said to her, but she just said, "Sorry Sheila needs me right now," and hung up.

It was as if my world ended right there and then. I was lost for words and overcome with total confusion.

I was at a loss as to what to do so I called my brother and asked him to speak to my partner to find out what happened. My brother did, but I don't remember what was said. Sadness clouded my memories of that day.

I flew to Dubai two days later to find out what was happening and to see if there was any chance of reconciliation. He said he no longer had any feelings for me. I called him a coward for breaking up with me by text.

Years later, I can see that there is no way of breaking up with someone that does not cause any pain. I may not have chosen to do such a thing by text, but it does not mean it is right or wrong.

I returned to London four days later thinking maybe there was hope. Hope is something that helped me cope. I allowed myself to avoid dealing with my feelings and accepting the situation.

I went to Sardinia with my girlfriend who had been with me on that dreadful morning when my nightmare began. It was helpful to be away in a foreign place where no one knew me.

I came back to London and didn't tell anyone about my breakup. Not my mum or my close friends. I had not digested the information and thought there was *still* a chance we would get back together. I slept on the sofa bed in my living room (I couldn't sleep in my bed) and woke up early to go walking or running. I did everything to avoid conversation.

After two months of surviving on three hours sleep a night, I went to see Mata Amritanandamayi Devi (Amma), the hugging mother. Here I met an old friend that I hadn't seen for many years. She noticed I was not doing well and we talked about the breakup. She mentioned that she was leaving the UK and heading back to live in Germany in a few days' time. She asked if I would like to go visit her before she left. I said I would think about it.

On October 26th, 2009 (my birthday), I woke up and decided to give her a call. I went to her house, and we had an emotional heart to heart conversation. She mentioned that she was learning something new, a new healing modality called VortexHealing® Divine Energy. Healing. I read the description of the courses and I resonated with the idea that we are conditioned to behave a certain way.

It suddenly dawned on me; my relationships and marriage had one common factor... me. I was, in some way responsible for both these relationships ending. I had to start looking at what part I played, instead of blaming others.

Yes, I had also been married ten years prior to this breakup. My husband and I had had a good marriage, as we were compatible and shared similar likes and dislikes. Then at a point, I decided the relationship no longer worked. This was a complete shock to my then-husband, family, and friends.

When I left my husband, I had felt very guilty about the pain and suffering I had caused him. Now it was my turn to feel this pain and suffering. I didn't know what was happening. I had no control, no tears, and no understanding. I was shut off from everything around me.

I was on autopilot, repeating patterns of behavior that resulted in two breakups, but I found something that showed me that it was possible to change. I realized that my old habits were no longer serving me. This was such a radical way of thinking.

Less than two weeks later, I attended my first class. After this class, I remember walking in Hyde Park, seeing a couple holding hands. Since the break-up, this would usually make me feel sad but it was different this time. I felt happy for them. Something inside of me did not see their joy as my lack. That was a huge shift in such a short time.

I had found a method that addresses deep-rooted energetic blocks and releases them. This was new to me. There was no hiding behind old habits and behaviors; I was facing them head-on. These releases created more space in my system and new ways of viewing life situations.

Although mentally and spiritually rejuvenated, the months between August and December when I slept so little eventually took a toll on my body. I collapsed the day I was traveling to Northern Ireland for Christmas with my family. My tank was empty, and I remember being carried into the car. The rest of that journey is a haze.

My mum was surprised to see me in this state. I just lay on the sofa, unable to do anything. I remember passing out in the toilet and my mum standing over me. I agreed that if it happened again, she had my permission to call a doctor. Fortunately, it did not occur again.

In January, the same friend that had moved back to Germany called and suggested I go for a walk outside and practice some yoga. My energy was still very low; however, I took her advice and went out just for a short walk.

It's amazing how being outdoors has the ability to rejuvenate our minds and physical bodies. It was not long before I was back on the yoga mat again. The transformation was almost instant. The energy was flowing again, and I was *feeling* again.

One of the side effects of this breakup and my shutting down was that my period stopped. For six months, my regular monthly cycle decided it could not function. The day my friend told me she was expecting her second child, something moved within me, and my period started again.

My friends all over the world were incredible during these months. My family in Northern Ireland supported me by getting me to participate in activities. They all knew that my world as I knew it had ended and tried to help me back to health and well-being.

Six months and many workshops later, I met a man who was a friend of a friend and had incredible intimate experiences. After months of being closed off, it was welcome. However, there was a problem. As nice as he was, this man was not available for a relationship. We discussed our feelings in great detail and decided until his situation changed, we were not an item.

A few months later, I was visiting friends in the US. Here I met a man I had known when I previously lived there. We had an affair, but it never went any further, for obvious reasons.

In September, back in London, I reflected on these two men I had met and thought on some level, I was attracting men that were unavailable.

My life was filled with feelings of guilt, believing I was undeserving, being a bad person, low self-worth and self-love. These kinds of feelings are the ones I had never allowed myself to feel or address. They had been suppressed in the past and admitting to them was hell.

Positive affirmations and VortexHealing® Divine Energy Healing helped enormously, as I could consciously focus on positive qualities that I knew I had.

Suddenly it came to me that I had to get clear on what I really wanted in a relationship. My previous long-term partners had been good people. I had just not been ready to fully commit to being engaged on a deep level.

I sat in a meditation and became clear on what I was looking for. I wanted to attract a man that was single, available, did not have children, spiritual, funny, physically pleasing to me, kind, and generous. I wrote these words down on a piece of paper and let it go.

Forgiving myself allowed me to open up and align myself to meet the person that I wanted to share my life with. My heart opened to vulnerability and being present in my emotional well-being. I took full responsibility for what I was receiving without judgment.

At the end of November, I was attending another workshop and had not intended to meet anyone. My friend from Germany saved me a seat next to her at lunch.

As we were eating, I heard the words "I am single, I have no children, and I am available!" I looked up! How could this be? No one else heard his words except me. They were the words I had written down describing the person I wanted to meet.

The following day the three of us ate lunch together. He sat down beside me and handed me a Coke. "Sharing is caring," I said, with a smile.

That evening the two of us we went for dinner together and talked like friends about our past and what we were looking for now. When we parted that night, he kissed me on the cheek. I felt 'trust'.

I had not been aware that somewhere along the way I had lost faith in men. He made me feel safe.

Today we are still amused at his words when we sat next to each other during our first lunch. The words came out of his mouth, but he has no idea where they came from. Divine intervention!

I am more aware of my needs and check in regularly to ensure that we both are getting what is best for us in this relationship. I express myself more and encourage this to be reciprocated. We are both conscious that we are not responsible for how the other person feels on those down days. We support each other through tough times with mutual understanding and love. Our happiness is not dependent on the other person. We laugh and enjoy being in each other's company.

We live happily together in a relationship that allows us the freedom to be who we are.

My advice would be to give yourself the time to get over any breakups and be thankful for all the lessons that relationships teach us. Be clear on the kind of relationship you want, and what is important to you. Harmonious relationships are developed through our own choice to have them; we decide how people treat us, and vice versa.

Susan Bock

Susan Bock is a leader in the field of creating transformational results for women entrepreneurs who are working too hard for disappointing results. Her clients include struggling solopreneurs and seasoned entrepreneurs wanting to scale their business up or down.

Her genius is helping clients navigate out of the quicksand of the daily grind that's robbing them of their passion. Using her Make More by Working Less proprietary program, clients discover the magic to monetize their genius, minimize the amount of time spent working, and maximize their freedom and fun factor!

Yes, you can have a business and a life you love!

Learn more about Susan:

Website: www.SusanBock.com

Facebook: http://Facebook.com/SusanBock.Coach.Speaker

LinkedIn:
http://www.LinkedIn.com/in/SusanBockCoachandSpeaker

Chapter 24

Happiness is an Inside Job

By Susan Bock

When I stopped believing what I believed, I came home to myself

I'm a self-assessment, self-help junkie – always have been, always will be. With each assessment, book, webinar or lecture, I learn something interesting, funny, intriguing or thought-provoking about myself. Now that you know this about me, you may not be surprised to know that I also love to ask questions – questions that are not expected, questions to discover, uncover, open up the channels to new ideas, concepts, and yes, beliefs.

The root of both 'addictions' is in my childhood. One of my earliest memories – around the age of four or five - is the feeling of not fitting in – like I didn't belong. I wasn't like other people. In my child's mind, the sense of not fitting in became the foundation for the belief that I wasn't enough – good enough, smart enough, popular enough, pretty enough, tall enough – you get the idea. Because I didn't feel good about me, I didn't feel comfortable with my family and friends, which reinforced my feelings of being flawed and inadequate. The pain, hurt, anguish and despair felt by that five-year-old can still be felt today as I write these words. At the age of five, I was bewildered; at the age of sixty-five, I have answers, understanding, and vastly different beliefs. Yes, its been quite the adventure with the lows including addictions, countless failed relationships, and clinical depression. The highs include celebrating nineteen years in recovery, twenty-nine years of marriage and being depression free for almost two decades. This was accomplished by taking the most frightening and fascinating journey of my life – the journey inward.

"Your task is not to seek love, but merely to seek and find all the barriers within yourself that you have built against it."

- Rumi

My need for embarking on the journey inward was selfish and self-serving. The tons of self-assessments I'd taken over the years was a result of the compelling need for me to understand me – to discover why I didn't fit in, and why most every aspect of my life was such a struggle. It started in grade school and continued into my professional career, relationships – including friendships, romantic, professional, and perhaps the most important of all – the relationship with myself.

The self-serving component was, quite simply that I was sick and tired of being miserable. When you don't like yourself, don't know what you stand for, have no idea of your purpose, it's virtually impossible to have healthy, lasting, loving, rewarding, fulfilling relationships with others – at any level. For my life to be different, for me to experience results that were different, I needed to change my behavior, and for that to happen, I sought, in fact, craved knowledge and understanding. I wanted a future that was bigger, brighter and better than my past.

Who I am today, how I live my life and what my life represents was what I used to dream about. Yes, I know, that's an overused expression, and yet, for me, it's absolutely true. Living, laughing and loving with ease, confidence and completeness still surprises me. I relish in the joy, simplicity, and lightness of being me. So, how did I get from where I was to where I am today? I want to share with you the three steps that brought me out of the darkness and into the light.

The first step was to actually tune in and listen to the non-stop 24/7 chatter in my head – to really listen to the words and question the truthfulness of what I was hearing. We all have one – an inner voice that expresses criticism, frustration, judgment, or disapproval of our actions. It might sound like, *You should. Why didn't you? What's wrong with you,* or *Why can't you get it together?* The actual self-talk is different for each of us, as is its frequency or intensity. When I really tuned into that inner critic, I was astonished at what I heard. The unrelenting message of *You idiot,* or *I can't believe you said/did/acted like that,* was alarming.

After listening to that voice for decades, it was a part of me... a big part of how I thought about myself, and how I showed up in the world. I was accustomed to the berating and each critical comment that reinforced my belief of being less than, not enough, flawed, unworthy and undeserving of happiness, love, and ease.

If you resonate with what I'm sharing, then try this for yourself. What are some self-criticisms that you are aware of hearing yourself say? Say it in the second person. For example: "You're such a coward. You're despicable, worthless. Be careful, or you'll get hurt." Or, "You should try harder."

How do you feel as you hear that? Get in touch with that feeling. What are you afraid of or what are you afraid of feeling? What are some authentic feelings you may be having about this situation that aren't related to shame triggers?

It seems that our society, school system, parenting, and business view criticism or guilt-induced comments as motivational.

Perhaps the thinking is that if you realize that your actions aren't good enough or ideal, you'll want to change. The critic in others gives them a sense of control by making 'helpful', yet critical comments to reinforce and control our behavior or control their feelings.

For me, the critic was the opposite of motivating - it was anxiety provoking and shaming. This molded my thinking and behavior into decades of anxiety, disease, isolation, addictive behaviors and clinical depression.

When I 'heard' what my inner critic was saying, really *heard* it, I sobbed with a depth of sorrow I'd never felt before. It was heart-wrenching. Gaining the knowledge that decades of my life had been ruled by my inner critic was sufficient to break me free from the hold it had on me. Sir Francis Bacon said, "Knowledge is power." I now had the knowledge and the power to silence the voice that was not supportive, motivating, inspiring or encouraging.

I had come to refer to this inner critic as my 'head committee'. What did I do? I decided to fire every voice that comprised the committee. Using the power of visualization, I gave each one a name and face, called them into my office, thanked them for decades of unwavering service and fired them. Boom – just like that, and it felt fantastic! Talk about a rush of power... it was awesome, and I can still feel the freedom that coursed through me as I write these words. Also, knowing that the critics would not vanish forever, I made the declaration that with diligence and intention, I would continue to 'hear' my thoughts, to be fully present, and mindful of my inner dialog so I could make a conscious decision about the voice or voices I wanted to hear.

What did I want to hear? I replaced the critics with cheerleaders – people (real or imagined) that cheered me on, encouraged me, believed in me and inspired me. It was quite surprising for me to realize there were numerous cheerleaders in my past – teachers, bosses, and friends. Those were the voices I wanted to hear.

The next step was a bit more daunting and, according to experts, is a most basic human need – that of understanding and being understood. For me, the absence of understanding and being understood was one of the many contributing factors to my depression. On a side note, did you know, according to the Center for Disease Control and Prevention, one in ten adults in the U.S. suffers from depression?

I suffered my first bout of clinical depression at the age of twelve. Because so little was known about depression at that time and certainly wasn't expected for a twelve-year-old, it was not diagnosed. Many factors contributed to my depression – of course, loneliness and lack of social support were the obvious factors, but the major contributor was that I didn't feel understood. I had no understanding of what was happening to me during this first depressive occurrence, nor did my parents, sibling or friends figure out what was going on. All of which reinforced the belief that I didn't matter. I felt isolated, ignored and invisible. More evidence and support to my limiting beliefs.

The universe has a way of working things out in life; things appear or show up for a reason. I was in my forties, in the midst of another deep depressive episode when what appeared for me was a lightning bolt of understanding and the realization that I was desperate to be understood.

Finding a person that was non-judgmental, patient, and empathetic – she created a space where I could express my deepest secrets and feel understood and validated. I didn't get any solutions, advice, or answers. Instead, she gave me thought-provoking questions like, "What does your soul really want?

What makes you happy? What are you grateful for?" And, "How can you forgive?" It was the first time in my life I actually felt like I was really understood – like what I had to say mattered.

Being understood immediately shifted my beliefs from feeling like I didn't matter to knowing I did matter; from feeling less than to feeling complete, from feeling inadequate to knowing I am enough, and most impactful of all: the shift from feeling hopeless to hopeful. Slowly, I was able to walk out of the depression and thankfully, I've not had a depressive episode in over twenty years. Amazing!

It only took me forty-five years to understand that I wasn't hearing or understanding myself, and the people in my life were reflecting my own inner beliefs. I had worked so hard to hear and understand others, and I fully believed that since I was good at hearing and understanding others, they should do the same for me. That never happened until I learned to hear, understand, and appreciate my own feelings and needs.

Today, my life is completely different. Sure, I love it when someone hears me and understands me - but now it's the icing on the cake, not the cake itself. Now I can listen to others from my heart and truly understand them because the child in me – my feeling self – feels heard and understood and appreciated, I can offer my caring and understanding to others from a full heart.

If you find yourself thinking, *I just want someone to understand me. I just want to be heard.* Or, *I feel invisible. I just want to be seen,* my invitation to you is to seek self-understanding by checking in with yourself. Are you aware of your inner dialog? Are you seeking to understand by asking questions or are you more inclined to make statements? Look for the meaning behind nonverbal communication like pitch, tone, and rhythm. Look for the hidden feelings behind the words to discover where misunderstandings can reside. Be curious and ask questions such as "How do I feel about this? How would I resolve this?"

The third step was the biggest step of all, and that was to appreciate who I was – warts and all. I remember a sponsor I had early in sobriety who, thank you universe, said exactly what I needed to hear. With compassion and from her heart, she held my hands, looked into my eyes and said, "You are not perfect – you never have been and never will be. So, when are you going to stop pursuing something that doesn't exist?"

She had me. That was the magical moment when I could release the belief that had held me hostage for decades and replace it with love, acceptance, and appreciation of who I was, along with the gifts, talents, and specialness I possessed. A sense of freedom and release washed over me. I felt like I'd finally come home by letting go of what I believed.

Forgiving myself for not being perfect allowed me to forgive others. For me, forgiveness and love are partners and only in the presence of these partners can I connect with other people.

As humans, we are hardwired at a cellular level for connection; you are worthy, capable, and deserving of love. It's when we appreciate our uniqueness that we can connect with others, appreciate their uniqueness, and enjoy the experience.

In conclusion, I invite you to consider this: in her most recent book, *Real Love; the art of mindful connection*, author Sharon Salzberg shares her belief that love is not a feeling, love is an ability. This resonates truth within me. I didn't have the ability to love until I learned, yes, learned how to love myself. It was difficult, painful, like learning to ride a bicycle. It required me to let go of what was holding me back and embrace the unknown of what could be. I had to hear, understand and appreciate myself so that I could open myself to receiving love from others.

Today I can walk through life and truly be seen without hiding behind layers of protection.

Today I am whole, complete and connected.

My wish for you is this:

May you pay attention to what really matters to you.

May you find safety, peace, and happiness within your uniqueness.

May you come from a place of caring.

May you wake up every day with love in your heart so you can hear, understand and appreciate the remarkable person you see in the mirror.

Yael Sunshine

Yael Sunshine is a yoga therapist and teacher whose life passion is to share the love, joy and healing found in yoga so her clients experience greater authenticity, connection and well-being in their lives. Yael sees yoga as a practice that aligns the body/mind with the deepest knowing of self. It allows us to claim our purpose, passion, and presence.

Besides private practice, Yael has piloted the Yoga for Breast Cancer program at Nyack Hospital, as well as Yoga for Recovery from Trauma and Addiction classes. Her integrative and innovative method of healing addresses the need of each client to be seen as a whole person.

Learn more about Yael:

Website: https://www.sundariwellness.com/

Facebook: https://www.facebook.com/SundariWellness/

Instagram: https://www.instagram.com/yaelsundari/

Chapter 25

Water Over Stones

By Yael Sunshine

The rain was coming down in a curtain of water, dense and gray. I smelled the spring rain full of possibilities, the green birthing of the earth. I was driving the winding path of the Sprain Brook Parkway to work. My thoughts jumbled, my body tightly corked. There was no more room to hold the pain and grief in my life.

I was unraveling. Unraveling a life of isolation, fierce independence, and too much responsibility as a single mother. Unraveling self-righteousness and know-it-all-ism, relying on my intellect to avoid my feelings. Unraveling all the ways I used my struggle to get my needs met and disempower myself. Unraveling my escapism into the spiritual so as not to feel the pain of my life. Unraveling what it means to be a strong woman afraid to reveal my vulnerable, tender heart.

After two years in Al-Anon (a twelve-step program for family members of addicts), I was finally working the steps with a sponsor. It was a tremendous shift for me. I had to admit that I couldn't do it alone. I had to let go of my ego to really listen to another person, and take in what they were saying. I had to learn to breathe every time I wanted to lash out when I was given feedback that triggered me when I desperately wanted to be 'right'. I had to learn the power of silence and not always having an answer. I had to learn the power of pausing and not knowing.

In Step One, 'We admitted we were powerless over addiction (or somebody else's), and our lives had become unmanageable'. For weeks, I had been examining the myriad ways I tried to direct my life, all the way back to being a small three-year-old child trying to navigate what was happening around me as my parents divorced and my once safe world fell apart. As I grew increasingly committed to the process, more and more was revealed to me.

I began unwrapping all the self-destructive, disempowering methods I used to manage my life. I recognized my desire to control myself along with the people and situations around me. I started to see underlying beliefs about the world and myself. *I need to selflessly give in order to be loved. My needs are not important. I must bear whatever happens to me. I have no say or choice about how my life is going. Who I am is unlovable.* How limited my life was because I believed all this was true!

The deeper I dug to uncover the mistaken beliefs that were making my life unmanageable, the more I uprooted my false self. I began to understand these beliefs as separate from the essence of my soul. Removing these erroneous concepts wasn't like brushing the dust off my surface. They were threads that were woven into the very fiber of my being. I was unraveling the cloth of self, pulling it apart thread by thread so that a new, more beautiful and true fabric could be created.

This experience was hellish. If I wasn't these beliefs, and they weren't true, then who was I? They were so intrinsic to my existence; I didn't know who I was without them. The process of extrication was terrifying. It rumbled me to the very core of my being. There were days I felt like I was going crazy. *If I'm not this, then who am I?* I wondered. As excruciating as the experience was, I knew I had to go through it. The door led me towards freedom.

I persisted through the devastating unraveling because I had a profound commitment to reclaiming the unsaid, but deeply knowing part of my soul. I held onto an intuitive wisdom that in order to fully blossom, we must dissolve everything that is not love within ourselves. It was this belief that gave me the strength to endure the process.

On that torrential, rainy day, I started to sob and sob. A myriad of emotions started to well up, feelings that I had held back and squashed down for over fifty years. The dam had burst. All the pain I had been holding tight in my being, the pain so great I feared I would die if I felt it, ruptured in a flood of tears.

I pulled off at the next exit and found the nearest parking lot. What came out were the tears and pain of my children's addiction. The pain of being a single mother, being alone, the financial struggle, difficulties with my ex, and of wanting something so much more for my children. I wailed out all the ways I protected my heart and hid my love, how I held myself back through not seeing my own light, believing myself as small, unlovable or not enough.

I called my sponsor, a loving witness who held my pain. As I sat there on the phone with her, I cried and cried. My body was overtaken with weeping; I became nothing but tears. I must have cried out the past fifty years' worth of sadness, grief, and despair. It was so pervasive in my body, so overwhelming, that there was barely any thought, just raw emotion. Yet it was a tidal wave of change.

I got home that day and decided to practice exquisite self-care. I made a beautiful dinner for my daughter and me. Within hours, I was in the bathroom, vomiting violently with a kidney stone. I suffered with them before and knew the unmistakable pain. I must have spent the next two or three hours on the bathroom floor.

Finally, at one or two in the morning, I was able to get up and knock on my daughter's bedroom door. Her boyfriend woke up and drove me to the hospital. When we got there, I thought, *Ok, he's going to drop me off. I'm a big girl. I can be here by myself.* Folded over, I arrived at the emergency room.

A few hours later, around seven in the morning, I woke up in a pain killer daze to see a shining face looking at me. "Why are you here? I thought you went home to sleep?" I asked. "I've been in the waiting room the entire time because I couldn't bear the thought of you going through this alone," he replied. It was such a profound moment of healing for me, seeing that caring and compassion can come from unexpected places.

I've led so much of my life thinking that I have to do everything alone, that there's really no help or recourse for me other than myself. Here was someone offering tender loving kindness, I felt such a sense of gratitude and an awakening trust. I now know I am always being provided for and taken care of.

Crying out, wailing those tears, and vomiting out my insides had cleansed me from what had calcified within me. A kidney stone is a powerful symbol for all the things in ourselves that have turned to stone and are no longer soft and yielding. I realized that I had been living in a metaphoric desert. The way towards healing my body and spirit was through the holy water of tears and the holy drinking of water as an opening to truly feeling Higher Power in my life.

Compiled by Dana Zarcone

So much of the Twelve Steps is about learning that there is a different way of living, a way that allows me to open to the power of receiving and trusting the flow and grace of life. I had managed for so long thinking I could do it alone. Finally, I had a sponsor, a community and a reawakening connection to Higher Power.

I've always been a person who's been deeply spiritual, yet I had felt disconnected from the Divine as a living presence in my life. I was practicing yoga and reading inspirational texts, but I wasn't open to receiving Divine love and grace or much of anything at all; then I was given the offering.

A couple of days after my kidney stone event, I walked into the local Starbucks early in the morning. Two very dear friends were sitting at a table. These are holy women who really nourish their connection to the sacred. They warmly invited me to sit with them. They were learning a text written by the Piaseczner Rebbe, the Rabbi of the Warsaw Ghetto, called *Conscious Community*.

The chapter we read was about understanding the simple truth. I was amazed at the parallels between what the Rebbe was saying and what I was learning about living the Twelve Steps. How do we reveal, deepen and strengthen our consciousness? When we let go of intellectually experiencing God, we have a soul return to our essence. When we 'Let go and Let God', we are open to Divine flow. We can live in Divine purpose.

As I sat reading and sharing these words and ideas with my soul sisters, I found my eyes full of tears again. Bathing in the wise and generous words of the Rebbe, I knew in my heart that Higher Power had brought me here to see the interconnectedness and abundance that had been present in my life all along. The spiritual connection that I had longed for was right here. I felt watered by truth and beauty.

As we finished learning, one of my friends turned to me and said, "We've been inviting you for a year and a half. Are you ready to learn with us every week?" I knew I had come home. Home to a connection with the sacred, home to learning how to receive, and home to recognizing all the ways my life is full of grace.

I know that my journey of pain was there to give me wisdom and connection. So many people suffer from disconnection from themselves, each other and the Divine. It is the unspoken thread of longing in our lives. I now feel an incredible commitment to standing in my purpose as a healer, mother, lover and beloved, daughter, sister, teacher, and friend. Sometimes the most hellish night of one's life can wash you free, like water over stones.

The way of love is not

a subtle argument.

the door there is devastation.

Birds make great sky circles

of their freedom.

How do they learn it?

They fall, and falling,

they're given wings.

-Mevlana Jalal ad-Din Rumi (translated by Coleman Barks)

Conclusion

So, there you have it! Raw and real stories from amazing people who experienced burnouts, breakdowns and – ultimately – breakthroughs. I'm very proud of every author that contributed to this book. The level of vulnerability I've seen has been nothing short of amazing!

So many of them got raw and real - exposing their underbellies so you can learn from their experiences. Some of these authors revealed parts of themselves they never shared before. In part, it was because they knew that it would help them in their own healing process. However, they also wanted to inspire you.

They wanted to show you that we all go through really tough, challenging times. It's not that we have problems, or go through challenging times; it's the lessons we learn along the way that matter.

It is my hope that you found a little bit of yourself in each of these stories, and you realize that you too can move from burnouts and breakdowns to breakthroughs.

If you enjoyed this book, we'd all appreciate it if you'd hop on over to Amazon and write a review. This way the authors will know they did indeed have an impact! Thank you in advance for your support on this journey!

Remember, at the end of the day, in order to live your life all in and full out, *Your Shift Matters*!

Dana Zarcone

The 'Liberating Leadership Coach'

Coach | Trainer | Best-Selling Author | Publisher | Speaker

www.danazarcone.com

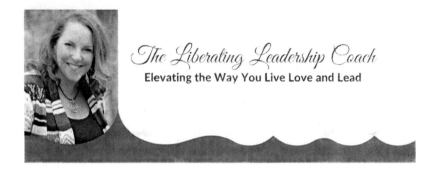

The Liberating Leadership Coach
Elevating the Way You Live Love and Lead

You are a leader! You may be leading a company or organization, a little league team, a PTO, your family or, simply, your life. Either way, you are a leader! The question then is are you a good leader?

Maybe you're a passionate, intelligent person but you're feeling stuck, frustrated, stressed, depressed or overwhelmed? Or, perhaps you're a manager who is having trouble motivating your team and, as a result, morale is low while absenteeism and presenteeism is at an all time high. Maybe you're a healer, coach, author, speaker or coach that is paralyzed by procrastination, lack of confidence and self-doubt.

Step into your role as a leader with courage, confidence and clarity!

We help our clients with:

- Up-Leveling Your Role as a Leader and Leader Developer

- Improving Individual and Team Morale and Performance

- Building a Successful Coaching Business

- Reducing Stress / Boosting Mental Health Wellness

- Discovering Your Life's Purpose / Owning Your Genius

If you're ready to elevate the way you live, love and lead visit www.DanaZarcone.com today!

Compiled by Dana Zarcone

THE END

CPSIA information can be obtained
at www.ICGtesting.com
Printed in the USA
LVOW07s0707280917
550387LV00028B/259/P